THE MODERN GIRL'S
GUIDE TO HATMAKING

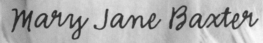

Mary Jane Baxter

THE MODERN GIRL'S GUIDE TO HATMAKING

FABULOUS HATS & HEADBANDS
TO FASHION AT HOME

Photographs by Claire Richardson

KYLE BOOKS

Published in Great Britain in 2013
by Kyle Books
67–69 Whitfield Street
London W1T 4HF
www.kylebooks.com

ISBN: 9780857830876

10 9 8 7 6 5 4 3 2 1

Photography: Claire Richardson
Illustrations: Esther Coombs
Design: Helen Bratby
Styling: Leida Nassir-Pour
Project editor: Sophie Allen
Copy editor: Barbara Bonser
Production: Gemma John and Nic Jones

A CIP record for this title is available from the British Library.

Colour reproduction by Scanhouse
Printed and bound in Hong Kong by 1010 Printing Group Ltd

* except for page 6: Lady with a Red Hat, Strang, William / Art Gallery and Museum, Kelvingrove, Glasgow, Scotland / © Culture and Sport Glasgow (Museums) / The Bridgeman Art Library
and page 11: picture supplied courtesy of the *Luton News* and *Luton Culture*

CONTENTS

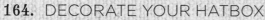

milliner *noun* a person who designs, makes, trims, or sells women's hats.

A milliner's tale

I FIRST STARTED MAKING HATS BECAUSE I WANTED TO BE SOMEONE ELSE. I LONGED TO INHABIT A MORE GLAMOROUS AND ROMANTIC ERA – ONE IN WHICH DRESSING UP WAS DE RIGUEUR. MY INSPIRATION INITIALLY CAME BY WAY OF A STUDENT DRAMA POSTER FEATURING THE BLOOMSBURY WRITER AND GARDENER VITA SACKVILLE-WEST. SHE WAS WEARING A WIDE-BRIMMED RED HAT, AND LOOKED THE VERY PICTURE OF LITERARY CHIC. I DECIDED I JUST HAD TO HAVE THAT LOOK.

I BOUGHT SOME FABRIC, GOT OUT MY SEWING MACHINE AND ATTEMPTED TO FASHION SOMETHING RESEMBLING VITA'S HAT. I CAN'T SAY MY OWN VERSION WAS A COMPLETE SUCCESS AS BACK THEN I DIDN'T REALLY KNOW MUCH ABOUT MILLINERY. BUT AS I CYCLED OFF TO LECTURES IN MY BILLOWING UNDERGRADUATE GOWN AND HEAD-TURNING HAT, I FELT ON TOP OF THE WORLD!

I CARRIED ON MAKING HATS, AND BACK HOME DURING THE STUDENT VACATIONS I'D DISPLAY MY WARES IN MY PARENTS' LITTLE GIFT SHOP IN SOUTH WALES. MY MUM PUT THEM IN THE WINDOW, WHERE I'D OCCASIONALLY CATCH A CUSTOMER POINTING HAPPILY AT ONE OF MY CREATIONS. I SOLD QUITE A FEW HATS IN THOSE EARLY DAYS, BUT A CAREER AS A MILLINER DIDN'T SEEM A REALISTIC WAY OF EARNING A LIVING, SO I EVENTUALLY BECAME A JOURNALIST AND WENT TO WORK ABROAD. WHEREVER I TRAVELLED MY SEWING MACHINE CAME WITH ME AND I CARRIED ON MAKING HATS IN MY SPARE TIME. MY UNUSUAL HOBBY ALWAYS SEEMED TO INTRIGUE PEOPLE. GREAT FUN WAS HAD WITH FRIENDS ARRANGING 'PHOTO SHOOTS' – THINLY VEILED EXCUSES TO DRESS UP AND WEAR HATS!

BY THE TIME I REACHED MY EARLY THIRTIES I HAD A DEMANDING JOB AND WAS BEGINNING TO FEEL FRUSTRATED THAT I NO LONGER HAD THE CHANCE TO DO ANYTHING CREATIVE. MY SEWING MACHINE SAT IN A CORNER UNLOVED AND UNUSED.

I'M NOT QUITE SURE HOW I FINALLY REACHED THE DECISION, BUT ONE DAY, MANY YEARS AFTER SPOTTING THAT POSTER OF VITA SACKVILLE-WEST, I WALKED INTO MY BOSS'S OFFICE AND TOLD HIM THAT I WAS LEAVING TO GO AND STUDY MILLINERY PROFESSIONALLY. HE LOOKED SOMEWHAT SURPRISED BUT TO HIS CREDIT, HE DIDN'T LAUGH.

THAT WAS THE BEGINNING OF THIS PARTICULAR MILLINER'S TALE. I HOPE MY BOOK WILL BE THE START OF YOURS. *Mary Jane X*

A HAT GLOSSARY

THERE ARE MANY DIFFERENT TYPES OF HAT, BUT GENERALLY SPEAKING THE ONES I'LL BE SHOWING YOU HOW TO MAKE CONSIST OF ONE OR TWO MAIN PARTS:

CROWN the top part of a hat.
BRIM the bottom part of a hat.
CENTRE BACK (CB) the exact back of your hat.
CENTRE FRONT (CF) the exact front of your hat.
TRIM the decoration on a hat.

Fitted hat
One that fits around the head and doesn't need any extra help to keep it on.

Pillbox
A small hat with flat crown and straight sides.

Percher
A hat that sits on top of the head rather than fits around it.

Half hat
Popular in the 1950s, these little hats covered just a small part of the head.

Picture hat
An elaborately trimmed wide-brimmed hat.

Cloche hat
A close-fitting bell-shaped hat popular during the 1920s and '30s.

Headpiece
Less all-encompassing than a hat but with more design and substance than a fascinator.

Fascinator
The name given to a very small headpiece, almost a hair decoration. They're often made of feathers and other trims.

Often though you'll find I use the generic term 'hat' to cover any and all of the above throughout the course of this book.

A BRIEF HAT HISTORY

There's no doubt about it, hats are back, and if you love hats, then why not learn how to make them yourself? You'll end up having great fun and saving yourself a small fortune, and you'll elicit admiring and envious glances wherever you go.

Hat know-how used to be commonplace. Turn the clock back a hundred years or so and you'd be surrounded by women who had millinery magic at their fingertips. Hats were the icing on the cake, the final fabulous flourish. You'd be as likely to leave the house without your hat and gloves as you would without your underwear! Most girls learned how to trim and update their own hats if not how to make them from scratch, and for young needlewomen, millinery was seen as a career with real potential.

Not only were hats regarded as a wardrobe essential, they were seen as a great morale booster too. In fact, hats were so renowned for their ability to cheer that they were one of the few items not to be rationed in Britain during WWII.

The bouffant hairstyles, mini skirts and general rebellion of the 1960s saw women rejecting headgear. Hats smacked of the Establishment and fell largely out of favour. A few brave milliners soldiered on but their clients declined in number. It was left to the Queen of England herself bravely to fly the flag for the British hat.

In recent years though there's been a remarkable turnaround. In the 1980s Princess Diana gave the hat a much-needed boost and now Catherine, the Duchess of Cambridge is showing a younger generation just how becoming hats can be. The explosion of interest in all things vintage has put headgear firmly back on the fashion map. Bright young things relish the retro look, and there's no better way of joining in the fun than by sporting a sparkling little titfer!

LET'S GET STARTED

Buying beautiful hats can be an expensive business. The craftsmanship entailed in making something special means couture milliners inevitably command a high price for their work. But there are ways around this. You can borrow from friends, buy second-hand, or you can learn how to make hats yourself – and that of course is where this book comes in.

Let me just say right at the start though that this is not a traditional millinery manual taking you through the A-Z of couture techniques. Rather I've based the book on a series of imaginative and quirky projects that I hope will whet your appetite for more. I've included what I believe are a few essential skills and coupled them with some nifty little short cuts and designs of my own invention to help you get hatting in record time. Some classic milliners will be shocked at the things I've omitted, but my intention is to help you make lovely wearable pieces without much specialist knowledge and without spending lots of money.

I'm very inspired by vintage hats and it's the ones that were made at home that really excite me. I love seeing what people managed to do with limited materials and resources. These hats may not have had linings or have been perfectly stitched, but they still looked fantastic. It's this spirit that I'm trying to capture in my book.

SIMPLE INGREDIENTS

IT'S A COMPLETE MYTH THAT MILLINERS NEED LOTS OF PRICEY EQUIPMENT OR A FABULOUS STUDIO AT THEIR DISPOSAL TO FASHION STUNNING HATS. HATMAKING, LIKE BAKING CAKES, IS ESSENTIALLY A DOMESTIC CRAFT. YES, SOME PEOPLE WILL GO ON TO SCALE THE GIDDY HEIGHTS OF HAUTE COUTURE OR HAUTE CUISINE, BUT ESSENTIALLY EACH OF THESE OCCUPATIONS STARTS OUT AT THE KITCHEN TABLE. I'VE MANAGED TO CREATE HATS FOR HIGH-END STORES, THE STAGE, TV AND VOGUE MAGAZINE, ALL FROM A SMALL TABLE IN A TINY LONDON FLAT, SO NO EXCUSES PLEASE FOR NOT GETTING STARTED. HERE ARE SOME OF THE THINGS YOU'LL NEED IN YOUR KIT. YOU'LL PROBABLY ALREADY HAVE MOST OF THIS AT HOME.

Apron

It's best to wear an apron when you're steaming or blocking hats to prevent dye transferring to your clothes. Pins can easily catch in your clothing too.

A needle & thread

You can buy millinery needles that are longer and finer than other hand-sewing needles, but don't worry too much about what kind you use. When it comes to thread, you'll need something strong, so try using a thread with some polyester content. I'll often suggest using a double thread for strength as lots of hats need a good robust finish. A Stitch-unpick is a useful little gadget to have around for undoing mistakes.

Thimble

Using a thimble can be tricky if you're not used to wearing one, but you'll find that some hat-making materials can be quite tough. So if you want to save your fingers, then wear one.

Glue

Please don't think that glue is forbidden. Hat makers will happily use adhesive if it's the right tool for the job so in this book you'll find some hats that require stitching and others that need sticking. A good strong all-purpose adhesive like Uhu is a must, as is Copydex, the white rubbery glue that comes in a little pot with a brush. A hot-melt glue gun is handy for quick fixes and for attaching trims. If you can, buy the type that has a narrow nozzle – that way you can be more accurate when you're sticking things in place. Do be careful when you're using the glue gun as the glue can really burn if you get it on your skin. If you need to press things into place, use the scissors rather than your fingers. Always keep your glue gun on a plate or similar when it's switched on – and don't forget to switch it off either!

Elastic

Sometimes called hat elastic, this thin tubular type of elastic is perfect for keeping smaller hats on your head. You can dye it to match your hair colour so it blends in completely. It goes under your hair at the back by the way, NOT under your chin! See the Basic Techniques section for how to attach elastic to your hats and how to dye it.

Scissors

You'll need one pair for fabric, another for paper and card and a small pair for fine work. Nail scissors can be handy too.

Clothes pegs

Clothes pegs are really useful for helping hold glued items together whilst they dry and for hanging things up out of the way.

Paper and card

Make your patterns from newspaper or wallpaper or buy a roll of cheap wide plain paper – the type that's used for kids' painting sessions. You'll need

this for the hats in the Cut & Sew Collection. I've been known to make hats from cereal boxes in the past, and with this book, I'm at it again in the Easy Makes chapter.

Mirror

This is absolutely essential for making hats. You need to check your progress in a mirror all the time, preferably a full-length one.

Bias binding

Bias binding comes in different widths and is pre-cut on the bias (see Fabric entry below) so that it stretches. I often use it to finish the edges of brims as it curves beautifully. You can buy cotton, satin and even printed bias binding. Read about how to attach bias binding in the Basic Techniques section.

A hob top kettle and steam iron

These steam producers will help give shape to your hats and foundation materials. You can learn how to use steam in the Basic Techniques section.

Sewing machine

I don't always use a sewing machine but it's a very useful bit of kit. You don't need one with lots of fancy computerised stitches though; in fact I know lots of people who prefer the trusty old workhorse handed down by Grandma. If you're not sure how to use a machine, then get someone to show you how or join a sewing class – there are lots of them around now and you'll soon make a bunch of new friends. The main thing to consider when making hats on a domestic sewing machine is that you often sew through quite tough fabrics and a few layers at a time, so you do need something strong and robust.

Fabric

One of the most important things to remember when making hats is that they involve curves, so fabric usually works better when it's cut on the bias. Think of Madeleine Vionnet's beautiful bias-cut dresses of the 1920s and '30s and you'll get the picture. The bias runs at a 45° angle to the warp and weft threads of woven fabric and when you pull on it you'll feel a stretch. You can use it to your advantage when making a hat to get a good fit and it will also help you when making fabric flowers. When looking for fabrics for your hats don't choose anything too flimsy or too bulky. Good robust cottons and furnishing fabrics are excellent, and for winter, lightweight tweeds and closely woven wools work well. For fancy hats, look out for sparkly finishes, lace and a smattering of sequins. I often cut up old clothes to make my hats too. Also it's very important to remember the terminology: 'right side' is the finished side of the fabric; 'wrong side' means the back of the fabric.

Old hats

Look out for cheap felt or straw hats in charity shops and markets. You can take them apart, re-sew them, or make a new hat entirely from them.

Finally you should also buy:
a flexible tape measure, a ruler, a pencil, pins and tailor's chalk.

SPECIALIST ITEMS

Petersham ribbon

Otherwise known as grosgrain, this woven ribbon is often used to finish the inside of hats and is a very popular hat trimming. It comes in a variety of widths and is traditionally sized in inches. I've given the closest metric equivalent. Avoid 100% man-made petersham – search for petersham with a high cotton content as this makes it much easier to dye and to curve with an iron (see Basic Techniques).

Stiffeners

Sometimes you'll want to stiffen fabrics to make trimmings or to give a bit more substance to foundation materials such as felt. You can buy specialist chemicals for this purpose, but I use good old PVA glue – it's cheaper and less harmful to you and the environment as it's water-based. When you're using PVA as a stiffener you usually dilute it – one part stiffener to four parts water. However, you'll get different results depending on the material you use so it's always worth testing first and altering the amounts as necessary. Go to a DIY store and buy your PVA in a big container, it's much less expensive than buying a small bottle from a craft shop. Decant the amount you need into a jam jar with a screw-top lid. Label it carefully so you don't mistake it for milk! And don't worry – your PVA won't be sticky once it's dried.

Interfacing/Bondaweb

Bondaweb is the brand name for a double-sided adhesive fabric used to stick two materials together with an iron. It's a useful millinery tool, as is interfacing – either the iron-on or non-iron variety. Both products add a bit of substance to flimsy fabrics.

Millinery Wire

Millinery wire, which is available from specialist suppliers, is very strong and is mostly used to give support to the edges of hat brims or to strengthen trimmings. Unlike normal wire, it's covered with black or white thread that prevents it from slipping when it's sewn into place. Buy the firm type of millinery wire – you should struggle to bend it. It can be tricky to handle and shouldn't be used by children as when cut it's very sharp. Where millinery wire isn't necessary I suggest using use cheap gardening wire. It's thin and flexible and will do the trick for many trimming jobs. I'll specify when this can be used. See the Basic Techniques section for how to use millinery wire.

Blocks and blocking

There's a widely held view that you can't be a 'proper' milliner unless you have lots of expensive hat blocks – the traditional carved wooden shapes on to which hat materials are sculpted. Well, it's just not true. I'll show you how to use a polystyrene display head, a giant darning mushroom and a can of tomatoes as basic blocks instead. There's only one project in this book that relies on a traditional classic-shaped hat block and that's the Simple Felt Cloche. Certainly, if you take up millinery seriously then in time you may want to invest in a couple of more advanced hat blocks, but there

really is no need to spend your money on these at the start. Instead, spend time learning the skill of blocking in the Basic Techniques section.

Polystyrene display head

If you want to buy something relatively inexpensive to give support to your hats whilst you're making them, then get a polystyrene display head. They're very useful as you can pin things on to them as you're working so you can see how your design is progressing. As previously mentioned, you can use them as a simple block too. See Suppliers for stockists.

Millinery felt

Millinery felt is thicker than normal craft felt and can therefore keep its shape if you mould it into a hat. It's one of the easiest millinery materials to work with as it doesn't fray, doesn't need to be hemmed and steams easily so it's ideal for blocking by beginners and makes a great foundation material. Felt used to be made out of animal fur, but these days you can buy cheap wool felts too. It's best to buy felt that's already been pre-moulded into a rough hat shape or hood, as much of the hard work of shaping has already been done for you. There are three basic shapes: cones, flares and capelines. They sometimes come pre-stiffened and can arrive with no stiffening at all so it's best to specify when you order. If you want a firm finish then buy the former, and for a soft finish the latter. You can also stiffen the felts yourself by brushing the inside of the felt with diluted PVA solution. Allow to dry completely

before blocking. See Suppliers for Stockists.

Millinery buckram

Millinery buckram is an ideal found-ation material for fabric-covered hats. You can buy it by the metre in large haberdashery departments, but I'm warning you now, not everyone knows what it is! It's a robust woven cotton material that has been stiffened on either one or two sides. It's very malleable and can be steamed to take on whatever shape you need. You usually dampen it first with water by running it under the tap.

Fascinator bases

If you want to make fun fascinators these pre-made shapes are the perfect quick fix. The bases are usually available in felt, straw or sinamay. Use them as they are or cover them in fabric, and you can sew or glue-gun your trimmings straight on. See the Fast Feather Fascinator. Look out for little pre-made hat shapes – very useful if you need something in a flash, but ultimately more expensive than making your own hat.

Veiling

Veiling can give a really sophisticated finish to your hats and also adds an air of mystery. Vintage veiling is lovely – it comes in all sorts of patterns. Modern veiling is usually more standard and will normally be sold off the roll in wide strips neatly finished on either side. I usually suggest cutting your veiling into a narrower strip, so when you do, make sure the neatly finished edge rather than the cut edge is on display.

BASIC TECHNIQUES

In this section you'll find some of the techniques you'll need to know for the more advanced projects in the book. Practice makes perfect – and I highly recommend you try out these techniques before you use them on your finished items. Some are a little tricky to get the hang of but persistence will pay off. Nothing beats actually being shown some of these techniques, particularly steaming, blocking and wiring, so it's worth signing up for a course to help you really understand these processes.

The skills needed to make the hats in the book vary to enable both beginners and more advanced makers to find something to suit them. Some projects will require a dab hand with glue or basic sewing skills. Others need more specialist knowledge. In order to help you navigate your way around the book I've grouped the hat projects into four chapters.

Easy makes These pieces require an ability to handle glue and Bondaweb as well as very basic hand and sewing machine skills.

Hat tricks This chapter requires you to have mastered some slightly more fiddly techniques such as the ability to handle and use millinery wire.

Millinery magic I've included some basic blocked hats and a couple of headpieces which will really test your hand sewing and millinery skills.

Cut & sew collection I introduce the concept of making your own paper pattern on which you can base any number of fabric hats. These projects will require a sewing machine and a little bit of basic maths.

HEAD SIZE

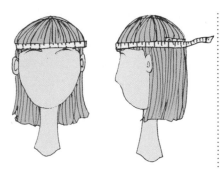

One of the first things you'll need to know is how to measure your head size. Many of the hats featured in the book perch on the head so don't rely on head size, but others, in particular the Cut & Sew hats, must fit properly. Take a tape measure and wind it round your head and then across your forehead at the widest part just above the top of the ears. Don't pull too tight – you want a comfortable fit. Get someone to help if you find it tricky to do it yourself. My head size is 22.5 inches or 57cm, which is pretty average. Jot your measurement down and keep it handy. If I refer to your head measurement during the project instructions, this is the measurement I'll be talking about. I'll call it (h) just so you're sure.

STEAMING

Steam is a milliner's best friend but it must be approached with caution as steam burns can be very serious indeed. Steam refreshes squashed trimmings like nothing else, and for doing this, a steam iron is usually all you'll need. Simply place your trim on the ironing board, blitz it with a burst of steam, then pick it up, shake it and hang it up to dry. However, to block and shape foundation materials into hats you'll need more of a constant steam source and for this I suggest buying a hob top kettle (an electric one won't do as you'll need a constant source of steam). Fill the kettle half full and put it on the hob. Once the kettle boils and steam is being produced, turn the heat down to produce a strong simmer. (If you're using a gas flame, make sure the flame doesn't come up around the sides of the kettle.) You're now ready to steam but don't proceed until you've read this safety advice. Keep your face away from the steam source at all times and NEVER EVER put your bare hands or fingers directly into the steam. Instead place the item you're trying to shape or refresh into the steam for a few seconds at a time keeping your fingers out of the way of the direct stream of steam. If the item is small, then use pliers to hold it in the steam rather than your fingers. Never allow

children to steam things, and never leave the kettle unattended. Make sure the kettle doesn't run dry and take care not to burn yourself when you're refilling it (use a tea-towel to wrap round the handle when you pick the kettle up as it can get quite hot).

Steaming is very satisfying, but it's quite a skill, so do take care when doing it. Lecture over.

BASIC BLOCKING

Blocking is all about sculpting your foundation materials to create hat shapes. Steam is essential to the process: the two go hand in hand. The most important thing when blocking is to make sure that your foundation materials (e.g. millinery felt or buckram) are malleable and moist so that when you pull them and pin them over your shapes or blocks it's not too much of struggle. Nine times out of ten, people fail to do this and it's much harder to get good results. You'll also need pins to block with. I'd usually recommend using normal household pins and a thimble for blocking, as you get better detail. However, if you find them too difficult to block with (and it can be tricky to get used to them) try using drawing pins instead until you build up your skills. When using household pins you need to press them into the block at an angle so that the foundation material can't slip up the pin. Drawing pins can be placed straight into the block.

TO BLOCK

1. Firstly, prepare your block (or whatever you're using as a block) by covering it in clingfilm to protect it and to prevent any marks getting on to your foundation material. Clean and clear the work surface next to the area where you're doing your steaming. Put on an apron.

2. Steam your foundation material until it's really soft, making sure you strictly follow the safety guidelines opposite. Don't let the material come into contact with the gas flame or electric ring or it will burn. Quickly pull and stretch it over the block, pinning as you go to keep the foundation material in place.

3. When pinning, always work with opposite sides: imagine a clock face and pin at 12 noon then 6 p.m., 3 p.m. and 9 p.m. and so on. This is one of the golden rules of millinery. Pin and steam bit by bit, and as you pin, pull and stretch your foundation material over the block so that it becomes smooth and even, working out any creases or lumps with your fingers as you go. You might need to lift the block itself into the steam as you work to ensure your foundation material remains moist enough to work with – but remember, keep your fingers out of direct contact with the steam itself.

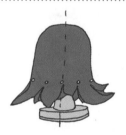

4. Once you're happy you have a smooth shape, leave the foundation material on the block until it's dry and can be removed. If you find it difficult to remove you might need to insert a narrow knitting needle between the foundation material and the block to loosen it. Remove any clingfilm.

WIRING

As you'll already have read in the previous section, millinery wire has to be handled with caution and shouldn't be used by children. However, if used properly, it will really help you achieve professional results. It's incredibly springy and should be stored securely on the roll so it doesn't come undone. Be very careful of the sharp edges and keep the wire well away from your face and eyes at all times. Use proper wire cutters, and put the wire down underneath the table as you cut it so that little segments don't spring off into your face.

WIRE STITCH

To secure millinery wire to your hats, it's best to use wire stitch, commonly known as blanket stitch. This stitch really binds the wire to your hat. Great care needs to be taken with the ends of the wire otherwise they'll work free and protrude through your hats and fabrics.

1. To work wire stitch or blanket stitch, first thread your needle with a double thread and tie a knot. Double threads can be a bit fiddly, but you must use a double thread to attach wire. Place to one side. Now measure the amount of wire you need, adding a further 8cm for overlap. Cut carefully with wire cutters and hold one end of the wire in position on the edge of your hat (or whatever item it is that you wish to wire). Keep the free end of the wire well away from your eyes at all times – if you're worried, put some sticky tape on the end of it while you work. Place the needle just below the wire and push through the material towards you so the knot rests just by the wire. Secure by sewing over the wire a couple of times.

2. Move 1cm along and push the needle through towards you again just below the wire. Pull the thread through, and as you do so you'll form a loop with your thread. Go through the loop from the back, pull tight and you'll have made one blanket stitch.

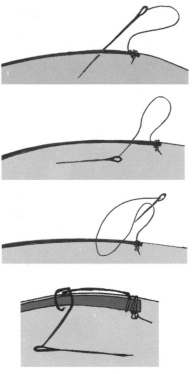

3. Go 1cm along again and repeat. As you work you can bend the wire with your fingers to help it fit the shape you're wiring. If you start running out of thread, just finish off the thread you're using, secure it well, and start again with another double thread.

4. When you get back round to the start, place the overlapping wire just below the wire you started with (removing the sticky tape if you used it) and blanket stitch the two wires down together. As I mentioned, you should have about 8cm overlap. Now go backwards, blanket-stitching the two wires together again. Repeat until the wires are attached very firmly to the hat.

5. Finish off your thread securely. For extra security, put a dab of clear glue at each end of the wire. If you don't fix the wire securely it may work loose and end up poking through your hat, so take time over this step.

JOINING WIRE CIRCLES

In a couple of the projects in this book, I use circles of wire. Here's how to make them. Cut your wire to the length you need, including 8cm for an overlap unless advised otherwise.

1. Thread a needle with an extra long double thread (about 90cm) knotted at the end. Carefully coax your wire into a circle and hold the two ends of the wire alongside each other so they overlap. Secure your thread to one end of the overlap by going through the loop of the thread with your needle.

2. Now leave your needle dangling and wind your thread diagonally towards the other end of the overlap keeping your thread nice and tight and holding the wires together as you work. When you reach the end of the overlap, bind securely a couple of times and then wind back diagonally the other way.

3. Do this again and then once more after that, binding at the ends each time. All in all you'll have wrapped the wire four times with the thread.

4. Now pick up the needle again and sew into the wrapped thread and finish with a knot. The wire should not be able to budge. For extra security, put a tiny dab of clear glue at either end of the overlap.

OTHER HAND-SEWING TECHNIQUES

YOU NOW KNOW ABOUT WIRE STITCH, BUT THERE ARE SOME OTHER HAND SEWING STITCHES IT'S ESSENTIAL TO LEARN. THE MAIN THING TO REMEMBER WHEN YOU'RE HAND-SEWING HATS IS THAT YOU'RE OFTEN USING MUCH THICKER MATERIALS THAN FOR CLOTHING SO IT CAN FEEL LIKE HARD WORK. I REALLY RECOMMEND THAT YOU GET USED TO WEARING A THIMBLE. HAVING A PAIR OF PLIERS HANDY TO PULL YOUR NEEDLE THROUGH THE MANY LAYERS CAN BE USEFUL TOO. HERE ARE SOME OF THE OTHER STITCHES THAT MILLINERS USE ALL THE TIME.

Some of these stitches will require practice – but it's worth persevering

STARTING AND FINISHING

Milliners like knots. Before you start sewing, make sure you have a nice firm knot at the end of your thread. Finish off securely by sewing two small neat stitches one on top of the other, then do a third stitch, this time bringing your needle through the loop of the stitch to make a small knot. Do this twice and then cut off your thread.

When double thread is needed don't try to thread your needle with two strands of thread! Simply thread your needle as normal and then pull the thread down so that you have double on your needle. Knot in the usual way.

TACKING

Always useful – tacking will hold materials together temporarily. Use a contrasting colour thread so you can locate the stitches easily when you need to remove them. Knot the end of your thread and go in and out of your fabric creating even-sized stitches of about 1cm in length. Secure by going over the last stitch twice. Remove by chopping through the stitches and pulling the thread out.

STAB STITCH

This stitch is widely used by milliners as it's almost invisible, which makes it ideal for attaching trimmings for instance. Push your needle back into your fabric almost exactly where you came out so you're creating a tiny stitch, but angle the needle diagonally through the fabric as you work so you progress along the fabric. This stitch is also ideal for hand-sewing bias binding on to a brim to finish the edge.

HAND-SEWN GATHERING STITCH

Although you can do this with the sewing machine, I think it's far simpler to gather fabric by hand especially for small projects like hats. Using a double thread, knot it, and work a running stitch (small evenly spaced stitches) about 0.5cm from the edge of your fabric (a little further in if the fabric frays a lot). Gather up the fabric evenly along the thread to the desired measurement. Hold the gathers by finishing as described in Starting and Finishing on the left.

ATTACHING BIAS BINDING: STAB STITCH & SLIP STITCH

Bias binding is a simple and effective way of finishing off the edge of a brim. You'll find it easier to use a slightly wider bias binding (especially if you have a wire on the edge of your hat). First of all measure the amount you need (leaving enough for a 2cm overlap). Fold in half lengthways and sandwich the brim edge in the middle.

Pin in position, placing the seam either at the back of the hat or where you know it'll be hidden under your trim. (If your brim is very stiff you'll need to push your pins through vertically.)

Now pull the bias binding around the brim of your hat, pinning as you go, keeping it nice and smooth. Trim back the overlap as needed when you get back to the start. Make sure you have equal amounts of bias binding on the upper and lower edges of your brim – this is really important.

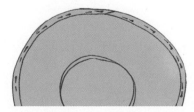

Tack in position. You can now machine-sew the bias binding in place with a straight stitch or sew by hand with a single thread using stab stitch or slip stitch.

Using *stab stitch* enables you to stitch down both sides of the bias binding in one go but it is tricky and needs practising. Thread your needle and knot your thread. Catch the top edge of the bias binding on your needle and pull your thread through so the knot is hidden. Now stitch back down into your brim 1mm above the edge of the bias binding. Push your needle diagonally through the hat and pick up the very edge of the bias binding on the opposite side. You'll have to twist your hat around to check that you're hitting the right place. Now push your needle back into the brim 1mm above the edge of the bias binding, slanting your needle diagonally along so that you pick up the bias binding again on the opposite side, about 0.75cm along from your first stitch. Continue round the brim with nice even tiny stitches until the binding is secure. Take out your tacking stitches.

Alternatively use *slip stitch* to secure one side of bias binding at a time. This technique is slower, but easier. Once again, thread your needle and knot your thread. Catch the top edge of the bias binding on your needle and pull your thread through so the knot is hidden. Now stitch back down into your brim 1mm above the edge of the bias binding but don't go through to the other side. Just slide your needle along under the bias binding and into the top layer of fabric until the tip of the needle re-emerges about 0.75cm further along. Pick up the top edge of the bias binding on your needle again and repeat the process.

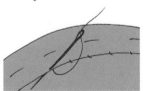

Go all the way around the top of the brim, then repeat for the bottom. Take out your tacking stitches.

MAKING YOUR OWN BIAS BINDING

Sometimes it's quite nice to use your own fabric as bias binding so you can match the edge of the hat to the fabric you've used to cover it. Take a look at the Beautiful Bow Headpiece in the Hat Tricks section (see page 75). You can buy bias binding makers to do this, or you can have a go at doing it yourself.

Cut out a long strip of fabric on the bias. You want to make the strip about 5cm wide.

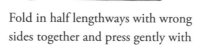

Fold in half lengthways with wrong sides together and press gently with an iron.

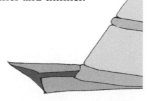

Now, open out and fold the raw edges into the centre, pressing as you go but taking care not to pull the bias binding as you do so, as it will get thinner and thinner.

You can sew individual strips together to make a longer piece if needed but do join them on the bias too otherwise it won't work.

DYEING PETERSHAM RIBBON

Cotton petersham ribbon dyes beautifully, and you can do it in small quantities on the hob in a pan. By dyeing the ribbon yourself you get subtle vintage-looking colours which give very pretty effects. You can save time and money by buying rolls of white petersham in different widths and dyeing it to order, rather than having to search out different colours each time. Follow the manufacturers' instructions on the dye for the best results. You can also dye petersham ribbon with tea or coffee to give a vintage mottled aged effect (see Elastic entry page 29).

CURVING PETERSHAM RIBBON

Milliners often finish the inside edges of their hats with petersham ribbon. This comes in many widths, but the one you'll find most useful for finishing the hats in this book is either 1.5cm or 2.5cm wide. Petersham will fit your hat better if it's curved slightly with an iron. Here's how. First measure the amount of ribbon you need for your hat leaving enough for a 4cm overlap. Place the ribbon on the ironing board and iron from one end to the other pulling the opposite end taut as you go and encouraging the ribbon to curve.

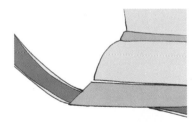

Sew into your hat using slip stitch or stab stitch, placing any overlap at the back of the hat.

FITTED PETERSHAM HEADBAND

Sometimes (as in The Simple Felt Cloche project page 114), you'll want to make a fitted headband that holds the hat in place on your head and keeps the hat from stretching. To do this, curve the ribbon and then wrap it around your head (with the widest part of the curve at the bottom) pinching together at the back. You're basically making your head fitting (h) in petersham. Sew the petersham together with a few small running stitches and press the seam open. The resulting headband should fit you perfectly.

Next fold the headband into quarters so you can see the fold marks,

then open out again and place on the inside edge of your hat (with the widest part of the curve at the bottom/open end of your hat). Pin the seam of the ribbon to the Centre Back (CB) of the hat, with the wrong side of the ribbon facing the hat.

Now match the front and sides of the hat to the corresponding quarter folds in the ribbon and pin in these places.

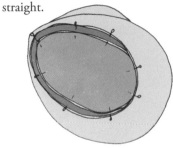

Continue to pin the ribbon into place making sure it's nice and straight.

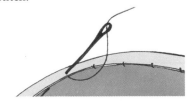

Sew in place using slip stitch or stab stitch.

CLIPPING SEAMS

When you're making the Cut & Sew hats it helps to clip the curved seams so that you get a good smooth fit. Snip up to within 1mm or so of your stitching line and repeat every couple of centimetres as shown here. If you're worried about snipping through the stitching, always sew a double row of stitches in areas that you know will need to be clipped.

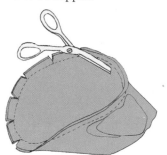

ATTACHING A HAT WITH A COMB

I rarely use combs but occasionally you may want to attach one to your hat to give it extra security or to create something that sits on the back of the head rather than in a forward position. Elastic doesn't work for hats that sit on the back of the head. You may also want to make a flower into a simple hair decoration and put it on to a comb.

So here are my hints for sewing on combs:

1. I prefer to use metal combs if I can, as they don't snap like plastic ones, but a plastic one will work too. Try to find simple ones with no ridges or bumps if possible – it's easier to attach things to them.

2. Use a double thread to sew on combs, and go over and through the gaps in the teeth in succession as shown. However, don't think you have to sew the comb along its entire length – securing the two thirds in the middle is often sufficient.

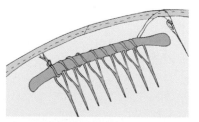

3. If you're using a comb in a hat, the comb needs to have some movement up and down so that it can be pushed into your hair. If you're using the comb for a trim, then the comb and trim must be really secure with no movement between them.

ATTACHING HATS WITH ELASTIC

Most of the hats in this book either fit the head or perch on the head in a forward position. Some of the perching hats are attached to a headband so that you can wear them very simply and with minimum fuss. Often people who are unused to wearing hats prefer this method as you can't really put the hat on badly. A slightly more sophisticated way of attaching hats is to use elastic – which is perfect for hats that sit forward on the head. Elastic gives a good grip, and you can usually arrange your hair to hide it. *Remember – the elastic goes under your hair at the back and not under your chin at the front!*

I've already described the type of elastic you should use in the previous chapter (see page 13).

As for colour:

If you're dark-haired buy black, and if you're making for a blonde buy white and dye the elastic with tea. Simply make a cup of black tea with boiling water and a tea bag. Leave to stand for a couple of minutes, squeezing the tea out of the bag to make a good strong cup. Take the bag out and put the elastic in, removing it once it's absorbed some colour, and leave it to dry. You can add a little bit of coffee to get a slightly darker shade for a brunette. This method works for dyeing petersham ribbon too.

To measure the amount of elastic required:

You'll first need to know where you're going to position your hat. Remember, it should sit fairly far forward on the head, or else it will slip off. Once you've decided on the positioning, make a mental note and pass the elastic under your hair pulling it up on either side to where your hat will sit. You want the elastic to feel fairly taut but not too tight. With experience you'll get to know how it should feel. Cut the elastic to this length plus an extra 4cm.

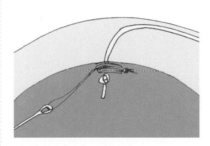

Now tie a knot about 1cm from each end. Pin each of these ends on to the inside edge of your hat, pinning behind each knot so that the ends of the elastic point inwards as shown.

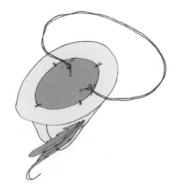

Where to pin:

For a round/oval hat or head fitting, use an imaginary clock and call the Centre Front (CF) of your hat 6 p.m. and the Centre Back (CB) midday. Pin the elastic at the 4 p.m. and 8 p.m. positions as shown. This usually works pretty well for most oval and round shapes – for other shapes refer to the specific instructions. Once pinned, try on the hat and adjust the knots and positioning of the elastic, if necessary. Remember, the hat needs to sit in a prominent forward position on your head or otherwise it will slip backwards.

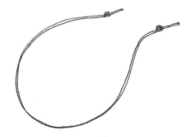

Sew the elastic on to the inside edge of your hat using a double thread. Sew over the elastic on either side just behind the knot (where your pin is) going right through all the layers. For this reason, use a thread that matches the outside of your hat. The knot should pull against your stitches so that it can't slip through. Stitch over the elastic three or four times pulling tightly, then finish off your thread securely. If you have a petersham ribbon in your hat, you can thread the knotted elastic underneath the ribbon to hide it. Sew on as before.

HATS & HOW TO WEAR THEM

The world is divided into two: those who love hats and relish wearing them, and those who avoid them at all costs. I doubt you're of the latter group if you're reading this book – but ladies, I'm sure you'll agree those 'other women' are missing a trick. As one of my favourite milliners Aage Thaarup points out: 'a woman can be dressed to the nines and be looking her most beautiful, but lacking a hat she will look unfinished. It is not just convention that she is discarding, but artistry too.'

Today of course, wearing a hat is no longer seen as conventional unless you're heading to the races, a wedding or (in some cultures) church. Women who wear hats for fun or simply to up the style stakes are perceived as being rather daring or even a little crazy. Well, the time has come to throw caution to the wind. By wearing a hat you create a unique opportunity to express your taste, your character and your sense of mischief.

One of the most common complaints from the uninitiated is that they just don't suit hats. I beg to differ. It's more a case of not having found the right hat yet. You need to try on as many different shapes and styles as possible to get your eye in. Only then will you start to know what really suits you. Only then will you find 'the one'. It's not really that different from finding the right man, is it?

I wouldn't offer hard and fast rules on what type of hat should be worn and by whom as sometimes style is attained precisely by breaking the rules. However if you're feeling unsure about where to start, here are a few guidelines to help you.

Members of my mother's family showing just how sytlish hats can be!

✳ When you're choosing a hat for a special occasion then if possible try on a selection of styles in a full-length mirror along with your outfit and your shoes. You need to see how all the proportions work together.

Two of the most common requirements are these:

To add height:

Try an upturned diagonal sweeping brim to lead the eye heavenwards. The trim should emphasise this line too. Feathers are especially good at adding height. If you're very petite, don't select too large a brim, or it will swamp you.

To slim down the face or figure:

An irregular diagonal sweeping brim (where the brim is bigger on one side than the other) will be the most flattering. The same type of brim will flatter a wider body-shape too. It's straight brims and straight lines across the face that you need to avoid. Cloche hats will only emphasise a rounded face and figure. Be careful with brimless hats; anything too small may look out of proportion.

✳ Masculine styles such as trilbies and caps can work really well on women. They're especially suitable for less formal events. Just make sure you get a good fit. You can always add your own trimming or just replace the ribbon for a more feminine look if desired.

✳ Think about picking out one of the colours in your outfit or complementing your eyes or hair colour with your hat or your trim.

✳ If you're going for a more elaborate hairdo then remember a traditional hat with a crown may not be ideal, as you'll end up with 'hat hair' (hair that gets flattened under the hat). Opt instead for a smaller headpiece that can work with your hair and not against it. Vintage hairstyles often look wonderful teamed with headpieces as together they give a very groomed look – just browse through the wonderful photos in the book for some great ideas. Stylists specialising in nostalgic looks are making a real comeback, so book in for a session. It's great fun, and even if vintage isn't completely you, you'll pick up some useful tips along the way.

✳ Think about how your hat will stay in place. If it's a fitted hat, then make sure it's comfortable and doesn't pinch. If it's a smaller hat then check that you know how to wear it. You need to be confident that your hat will stay put whatever the weather and however hard you dance.

✳ Smaller hats are often worn perched forward on one side of the head and usually look best worn on the same side as your parting (if you have one).

✳ Don't get hung-up on hair length. There's no reason why short hair can't work well with a hat. You just need to try things on to get the right look.

✳ Hats and spectacles can be a tricky combination. Frameless glasses interfere less with the lines of a hat, and upturned brims clash less too. Hats and sunglasses can be equally problematic. If you need to wear sunglasses then try to plan beforehand so you find a pair that works well with your chosen hat, or go for vintage specs and a sumptuous silk headscarf, which is a really classic look that seems to work every time. Don't wear veiling with glasses though – it's all too much.

✳ Your personality should match your hat. There's no point in wearing a hat that commands attention if being centre stage is the last thing you want. You're wearing your hat – it shouldn't wear you!

✳ Finally, if in doubt – remember the three 'A's: angle, attitude and attire. Fix your hat at a jaunty angle, pull on a fabulous frock and go conquer the world!

TRIMS & TOPPINGS

TRIMMING A HAT IS A BIT LIKE ICING A CAKE. YOU'VE MADE A GREAT VICTORIA SPONGE AND NOW YOU WANT TO GIVE IT THAT SPECIAL FINAL FLOURISH. FROM A BLOUSY BOW TO A FABULOUS FLOWER OR A SPRAY OF EMERALD FEATHERS, AN EYE-CATCHING TRIM WILL LIFT A QUIET LITTLE HAT OUT OF THE SHADOWS AND GIVE IT A STARRING ROLE. EVEN IF YOU'RE NOT MAKING A HAT FROM SCRATCH, SWAPPING THE TRIM ON AN EXISTING HAT CAN ALTER IT COMPLETELY. BROWSING THROUGH FLEA MARKETS, FAIRS AND HABERDASHERY DEPARTMENTS YOU SHOULD ALWAYS KEEP A LOOKOUT FOR BEAUTIFUL THINGS WITH WHICH TO ADORN YOUR HATS. YOU MAY CHOOSE TO MATCH A SILK ROSE TO YOUR LIPSTICK OR A RIBBON TO YOUR EYES. YOU NEEDN'T SPEND A LOT OF MONEY – JUST ONE SPECIAL THING CAN ADD THE FINISHING TOUCH YOU'RE AFTER.

YOUR FINDS MIGHT OFTEN LOOK A LITTLE SQUASHED OR BATTERED, BUT A FEW CLEVER TRICKS CAN HELP REVIVE THEM:

Crumpled artificial flowers can be very successfully rejuvenated with a quick burst of steam. Just place the flower on your ironing board and direct the jet of steam from a steam iron at the flower, keeping your hands out of the way. Pick the flower up and waft it around a little in the air – the petals will unfurl and open up. Hang the flower upside down to dry. Be aware that if the flower has been glued together, too much steam will make it fall apart.

Individual feathers can be gently washed in warm water and washing-up liquid. Use a hair drier to make them fluff up again. Glued feather trims, like flowers, are best just given a quick burst with the steam iron – they won't withstand water.

Ribbons can be washed gently in warm water – I often add a little drop of shampoo to the water and give them a final rinse in clean water. Hang your ribbons up to dry until they're barely damp and then iron them (make sure your iron isn't set too high) with a spritz of spray-starch.

There's great fun to be had in buying *ready-made trims* to add to your hats. Simply sew them into position with a few tiny stab stitches, use a dab of glue, or alternatively attach them to brooch backs so that you can pin them to your clothes too as decorative embellishments.

However, as well as hunting for pretty pre-made trims I suggest you have a go at making them yourself. To my mind, there's no better way to start out than by fashioning your own flowers.

Look out for:

STRIKING VINTAGE BUTTONS

LENGTHS OF PRETTY LACE

RIBBONS

VINTAGE FABRIC FLOWERS

UNUSUAL FEATHER OR

LEATHER TRIMS

VINTAGE VEILING

SPARKLY BROOCHES

OLD HAT PINS

SEW-ON PATCHES

COVERED BUTTONS THAT CAN

BE MATCHED TO YOUR OUTFIT

FLOWER MAKING MASTERCLASS

Flowers have been used to trim hats for centuries. There's nothing more becoming than a light-as-a-feather picture hat trimmed with a brimful of beautiful vintage silk roses. Creating artificial flowers is an art in itself. I once visited Legeron, the bespoke flower-makers in Paris, founded in 1880. Everything is made entirely by hand for prestigious clients such as Dior, Courrèges and Ungaro. I'll never forget entering the hidden courtyard on a Paris back street and winding my way up the creaking wooden stairs to the workroom above. There I opened drawer upon drawer of the most incredible flowers I'd ever seen, crafted from every type of material under the sun. I was enchanted.

I can't promise you'll make flowers to rival Legeron but I'm sure this bouquet of beauties will ensure plenty of compliments come your way. Some of the flowers call for stamens – you can find very realistic-looking ones on the internet. Just type in 'flower stamens' and you'll be inundated. You can often find them in craft shops and cake-making emporiums too. If you can't source them for some reason then improvise by threading tiny beads on to fuse wire – or use little feathers instead. I also mention floristry tape in this section. This is a slightly tacky tape which you can roll around wire stems to give them a better finish. You can get it from florists – but if you can't find it don't worry. Just use strands of wool or strips of thin fabric and wind round the stems instead and hold down with a little glue.

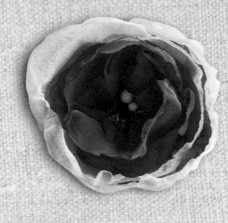

BURNT ORGANZA FLOWERS

THESE FLOWERS ARE INCREDIBLY SIMPLE AND LOOK VERY REALISTIC TOO. THEY'RE MADE FROM SYNTHETIC ORGANZA FABRIC, WHICH COMES IN A HUGE VARIETY OF LOVELY COLOURS AND IS VERY CHEAP TO BUY. YOU SIMPLY CUT OUT CIRCLES OF FABRIC AND SINGE THE EDGES WITH A CANDLE FLAME TO MAKE THEM MELT AND CURL.

YOU WILL NEED:

A candle, candleholder and matches
Synthetic organza fabrics
Pliers or tongs
Scissors, needle, thread
Clear glue
Beads and/or stamens for the centre of flowers

Safety is vital when making these flowers, so prepare well.

Don't let children use this method, and even older teenagers should be supervised. Never leave your candle unattended, and remember to blow it out when you've finished. If you've got long hair, tie it back, just to be on the safe side.

Set up the candle securely on your work surface. I suggest using the metal draining board of a sink, as it's fireproof, or perhaps use a metal tray. Have a bowl of water next to you, just in case your fabric catches alight and you need to douse it.

Always use pliers or tongs to hold your fabric in the flame and not your fingers. Finally, always test a small sample of the fabric in the flame first to make sure it will react in the way you expect. I found that tulle doesn't always work brilliantly, for example. As I mentioned, synthetic sheer organza fabrics usually work very well, but some give better results than others. Natural fabrics will just burst into flames – so steer clear of them.

1. First test a small piece (about the size of a 50p piece) of your chosen fabric in the flame. Light the candle and grip the fabric with the pliers. Pass the edges through the flame. Don't let the fabric linger or it will catch fire – you just want to singe the edges so they crinkle up a bit. If you're happy with the way your fabric reacts then cut out a number of circles of different sizes – small, medium and large. I suggest the largest of your circles should be no more than 12cm in diameter. Any bigger and they'll get difficult to control in the flame. You can cut them out quite roughly; precision isn't important with these flowers.

2. Now pick up a small circle firmly with the pliers. Smaller circles are easier to manage so it's best to start with them. Pass the edges through the flame. If you need to re-position the circle at any point, don't handle it as it will be hot, just release it on to the work surface and then pick it up again with your pliers. When you're singeing the larger circles, it's best to put your pliers right into the centre of the fabric – that way you have more control.

3. Once you have a nice big pile of crinkly circles, blow out your candle. Layer the circles up with the largest on the bottom and the smallest on the top – they'll sort of nestle into each other. You'll need anything between 5 to 10 circles of different sizes for each flower depending on how full you want to make them. Once you're happy either sew the flower together through the middle with a few stitches (make a cross shape with your stitches) going through all the layers, or put a dab of glue on to the bottom of each circle to stick them all together.

4. To finish, thread up a needle with double thread, and knot the end. Take a little bunch (about 5) of stamens and secure the thread in the middle of the bunch (you can go through the loop of the thread with your needle to do this). Fold the bunch in half and sew into the centre of your flower, securing with a couple of stitches on the back of the flower. You can also add cotton thread or wool to the centre of the flowers for a realistic look. Sew small beads or buttons into the centres as an alternative to stamens.

5. Stick the flower to your finished hat using a glue gun, or sew in place using tiny stab stitches.

BONDAWEB FLOWERS

LAYER TWO PIECES OF FABRIC TOGETHER WITH BONDAWEB TO MAKE NICE FIRM PETALS AND FLOWERS. THIS METHOD IS GOOD FOR FABRICS SUCH AS SATIN AND SILK THAT ARE DIFFICULT TO STIFFEN USING OTHER METHODS. I GENERALLY MAKE INDIVIDUAL PETALS AND SEW THEM ON TO A SMALL CIRCLE OF FELT TO FORM THE FLOWER. YOU CAN USE THE SAME FABRIC ON EITHER SIDE OF EACH PETAL, OR USE A CONTRASTING COLOUR. THERE'S A PETAL PATTERN IN THE BACK OF THE BOOK, OR YOU CAN MAKE UP YOUR OWN.

This method will make a flower similar to the ones used on the Fabulous '50s Percher in the Hat Tricks chapter page 84.

YOU WILL NEED

Bondaweb
Fabric remnants
Iron
Petal pattern
Chalk
Scissors, pins, needle and thread
A small scrap of felt
Buttons for the centres of the flowers
Glue gun

1. First iron the Bondaweb on to the back your first piece of fabric following the manufacturer's instructions. Peel off the paper and iron your second chosen fabric on top, making sure the bias (or stretch) of this piece of fabric goes in the same direction as that of the first piece.

2. Photocopy and cut out the petal pattern from page 172 and draw round it on to the fabric using chalk. You'll want five petals each of the large, medium and small sizes.

3. Once you've cut out your petals you can shape them with the iron. Hold the narrow end of the petal as shown and place the tip of the iron in the middle, pressing and pulling outwards to help curve the petals. They'll curve in slightly different ways depending on where the bias is in that particular petal.

4. Now cut out a small piece of felt roughly the size of a 10 pence coin, and thread a needle with a double thread for strength and put a knot at the end. Take one of the large petals and put a little tuck into the bottom to give it even more shape. It should cup gently. Sew it on to the piece of felt about 0.5cm in from the edge. A couple of tiny stitches should suffice. Leave the needle dangling, take the next large petal and again put a little tuck into it. Pick up the dangling needle and stitch the second petal into position with a couple of tiny stitches just next to the first. Repeat until all five large petals are sewn into position around the piece of felt. Try to space them fairly evenly if you can. Secure the thread and snip off.

5. Now you'll need to do the same with the medium petals. Thread up your needle again, then tuck and stitch these petals into place fractionally below the large ones to create another layer. Make sure you stagger this layer to fit the gaps between the previous one. Finally stitch the small petals into place to create a third layer in the same way. You might find three small petals is sufficient here. Use a thimble if it gets difficult sewing through all those layers of fabric.

6. To finish, sew a button into the middle of the flower. I quite like using the type of buttons you cover in your own fabric, and often use felt to cover mine. Finally, trim the felt on the back of the flower to neaten.

7. Stick the flower to your finished hat using a glue gun, or sew in place using tiny stab stitches.

COTTON ORGANDY FLOWERS

COTTON ORGANDY IS A SHEER, LIGHT-WEIGHT CRISP MATERIAL. IT HOLDS ITS SHAPE VERY WELL, SO IT'S PERFECT FOR FLOWER-MAKING AS YOU CAN ROLL THE EDGES AND THEY'LL STAY IN PLACE. IT LOOKS GREAT SLIGHTLY DISTRESSED AND FRAYED. IT DYES EASILY, SO I OFTEN BUY IT IN WHITE AND DYE IT TO MY PREFERRED COLOUR. IF YOU'RE CLEVER YOU CAN GRADUATE AND MIX COLOURS TO GET UNUSUAL VARIATIONS, OR SIMPLY USE TEA OR COFFEE AS A DYE FOR AN AGED EFFECT. I'M GOING TO SHOW YOU TWO WAYS OF CREATING FLOWERS WITH THIS FABRIC. THE FIRST DESIGN IS LONG, THIN AND ELEGANT – THE PETALS ARE ALMOST LIKE LEAVES. THEY'RE USED TO STUNNING EFFECT ON THE PRETTY PETALS HEADPIECE IN THE HAT TRICKS SECTION (SEE PAGE 88).
I THINK THE SECOND FULLER FLOWER DESIGN IS AT ITS BEST WHEN THE ORGANDY LAYERS ARE MIXED UP WITH OTHER FABRICS SUCH AS TULLE.

YOU WILL NEED:

The pattern for the type of flower you wish to make
Scissors, pins, needle and thread
Cotton organdy
Thin wire (long, thin elegant flower design only)
Floristry tape
Tulle (second flower design only)
Clear glue
Button for centre (second fuller flower design only)

1. For the long, thin elegant petal, photocopy and cut out the pattern from the book (see page 169). There are two sections (a) and (b). You'll need both to make one petal. Pin the pattern pieces to the cotton organdy on the bias. Cut out and remove pins and pattern.

2. Dampen your fingers and wipe off any excess moisture. Take section (a) and starting at the bottom, roll the edge of the fabric towards you, working your way up towards the tip. It's a bit of a knack, but keep trying and you'll get it. Keep rolling and re-rolling (you might have to re-dampen your fingers a little) until you get a nice smooth even edge. Now do the other side. When you get to the tip, roll the two edges together to create an elegant point.

3. Scrunch together the straight edge and press with your fingers.

4. Now take section (b). Roll the two long sides towards the centre using the same method as before. Bend over as shown (rolls facing outwards) and squeeze together at the bottom to make a little fan shape. Be careful not to squash the little fan flat.

5. Next cut 10cm of thin wire and bend over the end that you lay on top of the flower. Place the blunted tip at the bottom of the section (a) petal, overlapping the fabric on to the wire by 1cm. Now place the fan shaped section (b) piece on top of that and bind these three elements together tightly with thread. Just break off the thread when you've bound sufficiently and put a little dab of glue on top for security. Finish by wrapping with floristry tape as shown.

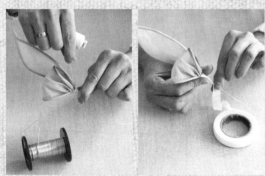

6. Create further petals in exactly the same way and then group together to create a fabulous trim. Stick or sew into place on your hat.

You need a little moisture to roll the edges of the organdy. I usually just lick my fingers, but (especially if you've used dye) I suggest you have a saucer of water nearby to dip your fingers into. You'll need to wipe excess moisture off though — you just want a hint of dampness on your fingers or you won't be able to do anything with it.

1. For the fuller flower design, use the pattern from the back of the book (see page 170–1) and cut out four large, two medium and two small organdy petals interspersed with four or five tulle petals cut out using the same pattern.

2. To make the tulle petals, pinch the tips together with a tiny dab of clear glue – this gives them a little more shape.

3. For the organdy petals roll each of the edges inwards with slightly dampened fingers as before. You'll find they go quite pointy. For a different distressed look, pull apart the edges of each of the petals with your fingertips to fray them slightly. Finally pull on the bias in each petal to help give it shape.

4. Once you've prepared your petals place them on top of one another, layering from large through to small and staggering the layers as you go. Mix organdy layers with tulle layers.

5. Thread a needle with double thread for strength and tie a knot. Hold the layers in the middle and put a little tuck into the fabric to give added volume. Sew the layers together in the centre with a cross of about 1cm, and pull tightly to scrunch the petals together a little more. Finish the centre with a button or another item of your choosing.

WIRE & ORGANZA FLOWERS

THESE FLOWERS USE SYNTHETIC ORGANZA TOO, BUT IN A COMPLETELY DIFFERENT WAY. YOU CAN ALSO USE TULLE. THE FLOWERS ARE QUITE STYLIZED AND VERY VINTAGE LOOKING.

YOU WILL NEED:

Thin but robust wire that holds its shape (I got mine from a garden centre)
Scissors, pliers, thread, glue
Some organza and/ or tulle
Stamens
Floristry tape

1. For each flower cut two lengths of wire about 15cm long. Bend over the top third of the wire to make a petal as shown. Dab the join with glue and bind with thread a few times before snapping the thread off and pressing with your fingers to make sure it's secure. It really helps to keep the thread on the reel as you bind holding the reel in your hand.

2. Now cut off a piece of tulle or organza and pull it over and around the petal. Gather the fabric around the join and bind tightly with thread, before dabbing with glue to keep the thread secure. Trim off the ends of the fabric as close as you can. Repeat for the other petal. Now place a stamen in between the two petals and bind all three components together with a dab of glue and some thread.

3. To make larger components, simply glue and bind each of the stems together, clipping the wire a little if needed to prevent it all getting too bulky. Bind in between the flowers with floristry tape or wool for a neat finish, bending petals out of the way as you do so and repositioning them afterwards.

4. These look great in their own right secured on to a comb (see Organza Flower Combs in the Hat Tricks section page 82) or glue or sew them directly into place on your hats as a trimming, taking care to clip off or bend under any wire stalks.

STIFFENED PVA PETALS

Stiffening fabric with PVA glue means you can shape it with a little steam to help create firm three-dimensional looking flowers. The drawback is that PVA can sometimes give fabrics (particularly satin and silk) a mottled effect and dulls their sheen. Organza and tulle can't be stiffened using the PVA method as PVA won't soak into the fabric. Most other things can be stiffened reasonably well. I like to stiffen little vintage crochet doilies and add them into the mix for fun!

You'll need to dilute neat PVA to stiffen fabric or you'll end up with unattractive white marks and cardboard-like fabric. I usually use one part PVA to three or four parts water, but you'll need to experiment to get the right mix for your chosen fabric.

The golden rule is to always test your fabric first and if it doesn't work, then use the Bondaweb petal-making method described previously (see page 38). Do be careful when you steam the petals. I've suggested you use a steam iron as it's easier to control than a kettle.

YOU WILL NEED:

Scissors, pins, needle and thread
The pattern from pages 170–1
A variety of different types of fabric
PVA glue decanted into a jam jar and diluted,
  plus a brush
Steam iron
Cloth or tea towel
A button or bead for the centre of the flower
Clear glue

1. Firstly photocopy and cut out the pattern from the book (see page 170–1). You should have three sizes of petal.

2. Cut out some smallish pieces of fabric and place on a plastic bag. Dip your brush into the PVA solution and coat your fabric. It doesn't really matter what side of the fabric you coat as it will seep through the fabric anyway. Hang the fabric pieces up somewhere until they become dry and stiff.

3. Now pin the pattern pieces on to the fabric and cut out five large, three medium and two small petals (or whatever combination you prefer). Place the fabrics on top of one another so you can cut out a few at a time.

4. Fill up your steam iron and switch it on. Place a cloth or tea towel on the ironing board and then put one of your petal shapes flat on the surface. Give it a good dose of steam with your iron, keeping your hands out of the way. Whilst the petal is still damp, use your fingers to pull and shape the petal. Depending on where the bias is in your fabric, you'll get different results. Lay aside and leave to dry. Repeat with all the other petals.

5. Now pile the petals on top of one another with the largest on the bottom and the smallest on top. Make sure each layer is staggered with the previous one so the petals are alternated. Thread a needle with double thread and knot the end. Holding the petals together, stitch through the centre of all the layers with a cross and pull tightly. Secure at the back. Sew a button or bead into the centre.

6. Try adding non-stiffened layers of tulle or other fabrics in with these petals to add textural interest, or mix in some cotton organdy petals. Pinching together the tips of your petals with a tiny dab of glue also helps give a different effect.

Chapter one

THESE PIECES ARE **EASY MAKES** AND REQUIRE AN ABILITY TO HANDLE GLUE AND BONDAWEB AS WELL AS VERY BASIC HAND AND SEWING MACHINE SKILLS.

YOU WILL NEED

Template from page 173

A large cereal box

Fabric remnant
  (large enough to cover
  your card teardrop shapes
  and circular base)

A small piece of strong garden
  wire about 18cm long

Masking tape

Stapler

Copydex glue

Bondaweb

Small piece of felt
  (to line your
  circular base)

Hat elastic

Scissors, needle
  and thread

Chalk

Glue gun

Iron

THE TRIM

I used artificial flowers but
you can trim as you wish.
Nothing too heavy though
for this hat.

TEARDROP EMERGENCY

THIS IS A STYLISH MODERN NUMBER WITH A SLICK COUTURE FEEL. IT'S MADE OUT OF A CEREAL PACKET, BUT GET IT RIGHT AND YOUR FRIENDS WILL NEVER GUESS! IT'S IMPORTANT TO USE THE RIGHT SORT OF FABRIC OR IT WON'T WORK PROPERLY. NOTHING TOO BULKY – CRISP SILK OR COTTON WOULD BE IDEAL. I ACTUALLY USED FABRIC FROM AN UPHOLSTERY SAMPLE BOOK.

Cut 2 pieces of card & bondaweb

TO MAKE YOUR TEARDROP:

1. First photocopy the teardrop template from page 173 and cut out two in card and two in Bondaweb. Make sure they're all exactly the same size.

2. Iron each of the Bondaweb pieces (remember to iron the paper side only) on to the plain side of each of the card pieces.

3. Now peel the paper off and iron your fabric onto the Bondaweb, pressing firmly so that it sticks.

4. Cut out each teardrop leaving a 1cm fabric border all round.

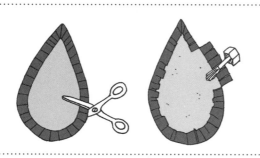

5. Now cut tabs into the fabric (go right up to the card) about 0.5cm apart – closer together near the point. Smear a small amount of Copydex on to the card and the tabs, let the glue go tacky, and then fold the tabs back onto the card really firmly so the fabric is nice and taut. Do the same for both teardrop shapes. Make sure the points are nice and sharp – no bulky bits!

Wire folded back & stuck on to back with tape

6. Take your wire and fold back each end to make a small loop. Use masking tape to fix it to the middle of one of the teardrops (on the back) as shown, making sure the ends are all sealed in with the tape.

7. Now cover the back of both teardrops entirely with Copydex, but don't go right up to the edges – the last thing you want is glue oozing out the sides! Once the glue goes tacky, press the two teardrops together really firmly. If you need to, place some heavy books on top to ensure a really good seal especially over the masking tape area.

Curving your teardrop

8. Once thoroughly dry, bend into the desired curve.

TO MAKE A BASE FOR YOUR TEARDROP:

1. Cut out a card circle and a Bondaweb circle 11cm in diameter. Iron the Bondaweb to the card as before, remove the paper, and once again press the fabric on top with an iron. Cut out leaving 1cm of fabric all round.

2. Cut tabs into the fabric as before, putting a little glue on to the edges of the card. Allow it to go tacky and then fold the tabs back and stick them down.

3. Once dry, cut into the centre of the circle, overlap the edges by 2cm and staple together.

Fabric-covered cardboard base is stapled together

TO FINISH

1. Using the glue gun, apply hot glue to the top of the base where your staples are and firmly stick the curved teardrop on top as shown. Try to do this as neatly as possible, and don't use too much glue or it will ooze out and spoil the finish of your hat. Press together really firmly. You don't want the teardrop wobbling around!

The teardrop & base are stuck together with hot glue

2. Trim your hat as desired, sticking your trim in place using hot glue.

3. Sew your elastic on to the base (see Basic Techniques to learn how to do this).

Position of elastic sewn on to the base

4. Finally cut out a small felt disc for a lining (using pinking shears gives a nice serrated edge) and use Copydex or hot glue to stick it onto the underside of your base as shown, covering the knotted ends of the elastic for neatness.

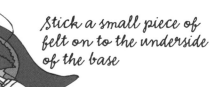

Stick a small piece of felt on to the underside of the base

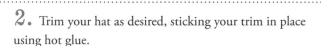

TREASURED TIARA

THIS LITTLE BEAUTY OFFERS GLAMOUR ON THE GO. IT LOOKS LIKE AN HEIRLOOM BUT IN FACT IT'S BEEN WHIPPED UP IN JUST A COUPLE OF HOURS. I LOVE THE TREASURE-CHEST LOOK OF THIS TIARA. THE ONE PICTURED HERE HAS A BRIDAL FEEL ABOUT IT, BUT CHANGE THE COLOURS AND COMBINATIONS AND IT COULD WORK EQUALLY WELL AT A PARTY OR OTHER EVENT. TO MAKE IT YOU'LL NEED A FABRIC-COVERED HEADBAND. MINE WAS SLIGHTLY PADDED, WHICH MADE IT EASIER TO SEW INTO. COLLECT TOGETHER ALL THOSE PRETTY BUTTONS, SEQUINS, BEADS AND BROKEN PIECES OF JEWELLERY YOU'VE BEEN HOARDING. IF YOU'RE USING OLD BROOCHES, REMOVE THE BACKS FIRST WITH PLIERS, AND MAKE SURE THERE ARE NO SHARP EDGES. (IF YOU LEAVE THE BACKS ON THE BROOCHES THEY WON'T FIT SNUGLY TO THE HEADBAND.) DON'T USE TOO MANY HEAVY ITEMS, AS THE HEADBAND WILL FEEL TOO WEIGHTY. JUST FEATURE A COUPLE OF LARGER ITEMS TO ADD IMPACT.
OK – *you're ready to start!*

YOU WILL NEED:

A slightly padded fabric covered headband

A collection of beautiful bits and pieces – lots of small buttons and beads, broken earrings or brooches etc.

Scissors, needle and thread

1. Start from the centre of the headband, and position heavier items such as brooches here. A lot of weight on one side will make the headband slip round, so some planning is needed.

2. Thread your needle with a double thread and put a knot on the end. Sew on no more than six to eight items at a time, so that if a thread snaps, everything won't come off. If you're sewing on an old brooch, you'll have to find ways of sewing around it and through it to make sure it's secure.

3. Keep trying the headband on and checking in the mirror as you work to make sure the headband is shaping up the way you imagine.

4. You're aiming for a really rich clustered look, so it's worth sewing extra buttons and beads into any gaps at the end.

BEACH BANDEAU IN A BAG

THIS EASY-TO-MAKE BANDEAU HAS A TURBAN FEEL ABOUT IT, BUT IT'S SIMPLER TO MAKE AND TO WEAR. GREAT FOR HOLIDAYS, IT COMES IN A CUTE LITTLE MATCHING BAG INTO WHICH YOU CAN POP YOUR LIPSTICK AND A MIRROR FOR ANY FINAL ADJUSTMENTS! YOU CAN MAKE THIS BANDEAU AS WIDE AS YOU LIKE. I PREFER TO MAKE MINE REALLY WIDE, THEN I CAN ALWAYS SCRUNCH IT UP FOR A NARROWER LOOK IF I FEEL LIKE IT. YOU CAN WEAR THE BANDEAU WITH THE GATHERS AT EITHER THE TOP OR THE BOTTOM.

T-shirt fabric is great as it doesn't fray and doesn't need hemming

YOU WILL NEED:

A large old cotton T-shirt
Scissors, pins, needle and thread, measuring tape
Chalk
Sewing machine
Piece of ribbon and a bodkin (large blunt needle) for the bag
Iron

TO MAKE THE BEACH BANDEAU:

1. Cut the front from the back of the T-shirt and mark out a long wide strip on one side with the chalk. The strip needs to be long enough to fit comfortably around your head leaving enough for a small seam. In terms of width, I'd suggest about 28cm. Remember, the material will stretch. Cut out.

Strip of fabric, right sides facing

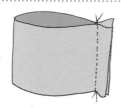

2. With right sides facing, pin together the short sides of the T-shirt strip leaving a small seam allowance. Try on for fit, and when you're happy, sew up the seam using a straight stitch on your machine. Remove pins. Press seams out.

Scrunching tube of fabric up & holding with pins

3. Turn the right way out and scrunch the tube together along the line of stitching and hold together with a couple of pins.

Small section with edges folded & pinned

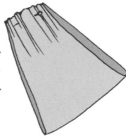

4. Cut out another small strip of T-shirt fabric about 7cm wide and 10cm long. Turn under the raw edges of the 10cm sides and sew each down using the straight stitch on your machine. Now fold the strip in place over the scrunched up section of your tube to create a little loop.

5. Pin one short end of the loop over the other, turning under the raw edge for neatness.

6. Stitch down with a few hand stitches as shown. Remove all pins.

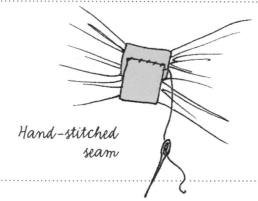

Hand-stitched seam

TO MAKE THE LITTLE MATCHING BAG:

1. Cut out two small rectangles (about 12 x 16cm) from the remainder of the T-shirt. Place with right sides together, and machine stitch down one long side, across the bottom and up the other side, leaving 3cm unstitched at the top of this last side. Leave the fourth short side completely unstitched.

2. Turn the right way out, press and fold the top unsewn edge down inside by 1.5cm tucking under the side seams as you do so. Machine stitch along the bottom of this fold to create a channel for your ribbon.

3. Thread a length of ribbon on to a bodkin and push through the open ends of the channel.

4. Remove the bodkin and draw up the ribbon to make your bag. Stash your bandeau and any other bits and bobs inside.

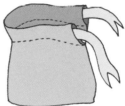

the little bag

FAST FEATHER FASCINATOR

FASCINATORS HAVE GOT A BIT OF A BAD
REPUTATION – LARGELY BECAUSE OF SOME
OF THE POOR-QUALITY VERSIONS AVAILABLE
ON THE HIGH STREET. IT REALLY ISN'T HARD
TO MAKE SOMETHING MUCH MORE EXCITING
YOURSELF THAT NEEDN'T COST THE EARTH
EITHER. THIS FASCINATOR USES PHEASANT
FEATHERS. YOU CAN BUY THEM IN BOTH
NATURAL AND DYED COLOURS, OR OF COURSE
YOU CAN COLLECT THEM ON COUNTRYSIDE
WALKS. IF YOU DO THIS, WASH THEM GENTLY
IN WARM SOAPY WATER AND LEAVE THEM
TO DRY BEFORE USING THEM. RUN THEM
THROUGH YOUR HANDS AFTERWARDS TO
PUT SOME OF THE NATURAL OIL FROM
YOUR FINGERS BACK INTO THE FEATHER.

*I'll show you how to curl the pheasant
feathers to make them look rather special.*

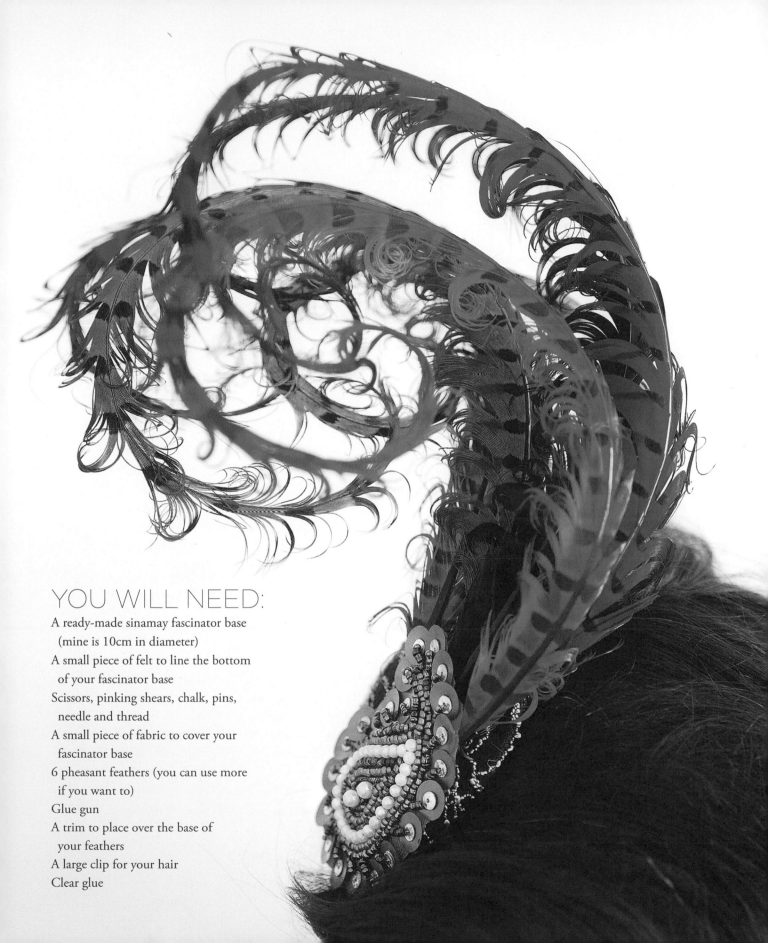

YOU WILL NEED:

A ready-made sinamay fascinator base
(mine is 10cm in diameter)

A small piece of felt to line the bottom
of your fascinator base

Scissors, pinking shears, chalk, pins,
needle and thread

A small piece of fabric to cover your
fascinator base

6 pheasant feathers (you can use more
if you want to)

Glue gun

A trim to place over the base of
your feathers

A large clip for your hair

Clear glue

1. Place your fascinator base on to your felt and draw around it with chalk. Cut out with pinking shears, trimming down a little if necessary so it fits neatly inside your fascinator base to make a lining. Lay to one side. You'll use this at the end.

2. Take your small piece of fabric and pin it round your fascinator base as shown. Stitch round the edge following the little ridge on the fascinator base (it's usually about 1cm in from the edge). Use stab stitches on the top of the base and stitches about 2cm long underneath. Trim any spare fabric back neatly.

3. Now prepare your feathers. Take a pheasant feather in one hand and your closed scissors in the other hand. As if you were curling parcel tape, gently but firmly run the edge of the scissors along the feathery pieces a section at a time from where they join the spine to their tips. You'll find that they separate out and curl. Go right the way along both sides of the feather from the bottom to the top until the whole thing is curled. Repeat for all your feathers.

4. Next, starting 6cm from the bottom of each feather, use the closed scissors to press into the back of the spine so that it bends ever so slightly. Move the scissors along a little further and bend the spine again. Repeat most of the way up the feather. As you work you'll see that the feather soon starts to curve. The more you bend the spine, the more it will curve. As the spine gets thinner it gets weaker so take care as you don't want it to break. When you're a few centimetres from the top of the feather you can run the scissors gently along the spine to make it curve more tightly. Repeat for the other feathers.

5. Stick the feathers one by one on to the fascinator base using the glue gun, taking care to get the angle of each feather right. You want the feathers upright, not flat against the base. Press each feather firmly into position using the flat side of your scissors and not your fingers. You don't want to burn yourself. Remember, the hot glue will seep through the back of the base so watch your fingers there too.

6. Finally stick your trim over the base of the feathers to cover any messy bits. Pull off any stringy bits of hot glue.

7. Take the lining you made earlier and cut two little slits into the middle. Thread through your clip (bending slightly if need be so that it fits snugly into the curve of your fascinator base).

8. Cover the whole of the back of the felt lining and the clip with clear glue. Allow the glue to go a little tacky and then press into position with the point of the clip towards the front of the fascinator (don't worry too much about this, as you'll probably wear the fascinator in all sorts of different positions). Allow to dry, then go fascinate!

TEA TOWEL TOPKNOT

HERE'S A WAY OF CREATING AN OH-SEW SIMPLE RETRO-STYLE TOPKNOT OUT OF AN OLD TEA TOWEL AND SOME GARDEN WIRE. IT DOESN'T SOUND VERY GLAM, BUT MAKE ONE AND YOU'LL BE PLEASANTLY SURPRISED BY THE MAGICAL TRANSFORMATION. CHOOSE AN INTERESTING TEA TOWEL – PERHAPS A SOUVENIR OR SEASIDE ONE. THE WACKIER THE TEA TOWEL, THE MORE EYE-CATCHING THE TOPKNOT. IF YOUR TEA TOWEL IS NEW, WASH IT FIRST TO MAKE SURE IT'S NICE AND SOFT.

YOU WILL NEED:

An interesting tea towel

Measuring tape

Pins, scissors, needle and thread

Sewing machine

Iron

Knitting needle

Some plastic coated garden wire and pliers/wire cutters

Clear glue

1. First decide which parts of the tea towel you want to feature and cut out four strips 10cm x 60cm each. Two strips will make the front and two the back of the topknot. If you want to make a shorter topknot, then make the sections 50cm long.

2. With right sides together, sew each pair of strips together along the short 10cm side leaving a 1cm seam allowance. Press seams open with the iron.

3. Place the two long strips right sides together and pin securely down the middle. Cut each end at an angle as shown.

4. Start to machine sew (using a straight stitch) right the way around the strip with a 1cm seam allowance but make sure you leave a gap of about 10cm unsewn in the centre on one side to feed the wire through later. Reinforce the corners with a second line of machine stitching and trim back the seam allowance at each corner so that when you turn the strip the right way out it won't be too bulky. Use a knitting needle to help turn the strip the right way out if needed and press flat with the iron.

5. Measure the amount of wire you need to go the length of the fabric strip, adding on an extra 20cm of wire at each end to make two loops. Use glue and thread to bind the ends of the wire down securely. Snip off any spare wire with the pliers. The wire should be a really snug fit for the fabric tube – you don't want limp bits of fabric left unsupported at the ends.

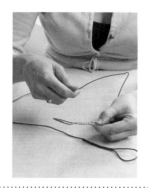
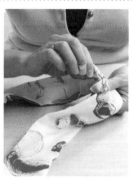

6. Now feed each looped end of the wire through the hole you've left and finally sew the hole up by hand with a few small stitches.

7. Twist into place around your head and experiment with different styles of topknots and bows. Straighten out after wearing and store folded into four.
You can also make a little bag to store the topknot in using the same method described for the bag in the Beach Bandeau project (see page 54).

A VERY VINTAGE EMERGENCY

THIS HAS A REAL '50S VIBE, AND SCREAMS VINTAGE.
LIKE THE TEARDROP EMERGENCY, THIS IS MADE OUT
OF A CEREAL PACKET. SHHHH – DON'T TELL ANYONE!
IT'S MILLINERY AT ITS MOST MAGICAL.

YOU WILL NEED:

Large cereal packet
Pencil, chalk and ruler
Scissors, pins, thimble,
 needle and thread
Copydex glue
Fabric remnant – large
 enough to cut out
 wide strips on the bias
 to cover your card
Iron
Knitting needle
Sewing machine
A comb to sew to the hat
Clothes peg
Contrasting fabric
 for bow trim
Iron
Glue gun

TO MAKE THE HEADPIECE:

1. Open out your cereal packet and mark four 46cm x 3.5cm strips on to the unprinted cardboard. Cut out, and glue each pair of strips together (if you're using a pale fabric, glue together the printed sides). Allow to dry thoroughly. Make sure you don't stick the folds in the cardboard on top of each other to minimise their effect. Once the strips are dry, run them between your fingers to encourage them to curve nicely. This is important as it will help create a smooth shape.

2. Mark out two 46cm x 9cm strips on to your fabric on the bias. Cut out and fold each in half lengthways with right sides together and press gently with the iron (be careful not to stretch the fabric as you do so or you'll make it too narrow). Put a few pins in place to help hold the fabric together and then sew down the long raw edge of each strip with a 0.5cm seam allowance. Be very careful with this seam – you're going to need to push the card strips down through the tubes you're making so take care not to make these tubes too narrow. Turn the tubes the right way out, using a knitting needle to help you.

3. Take your first card strip and pull the first tube of fabric over it. Don't worry if it's a bit baggy. Try and line up the seam with the edge of the card if you can – it's just a bit neater. Now machine sew one end of the strip going through both fabric and card. The machine should do this happily but use a slightly longer stitch than normal. Trim to neaten.

4. Pull the fabric taut, hold it in place with your fingers and machine sew up the other end. Trim again to neaten. Do the same with the second card strip. You'll find the strips naturally curve one way, so use this natural curve to create two separate loops, holding each in place by machine sewing the ends down. (You can also glue the ends together if you prefer.)

5. Take your comb and hand sew it into place as shown on to one of the loops, sewing only the central portion of the comb down so it can move around a little. Now glue the second loop in place on top of the first. Hold the two pieces together, with a clothes peg if need be, until completely dry.

 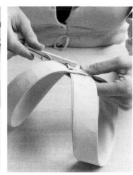

TO MAKE THE BOW:

1. 1. Cut a strip of fabric (don't worry about the bias) 85 x 14cm. Fold in half right sides together and chop the ends on the diagonal. Pin to hold the fabric in place and sew around the seams leaving one end open. Now trim and clip the seam at the corners, then use a knitting needle to help you turn the tube the right way out. Press flat and sew up the open end neatly by hand using slip stitch.

2. Thread up a needle with a double thread and put a knot at the end. Fold a loop into the bow about 14cm from the end (the loop is about 20cm long in total). Put a little tuck into the fabric from left to right and hold the tuck in place with a couple of tiny stitches. Bring your needle out at the back. Now fold another loop (a little larger) on top of the first, pushing this loop slightly to the right. Again put in a little tuck and hold with a couple of tiny stitches. Bring your needle out at the front. Tuck the remaining tail over to the back, pushing both the tails to the left and the loops to the right. Stab stitch to hold this position. Finally, fold over the side of the top loop and hold with a stab stitch. Glue gun the bow into position as shown with the loops and tails facing forwards.

When wearing this headpiece you need to push the comb forward into your hair. It will probably work best with up-do's.

GLITZY GLAM HEADBANDS

THESE HEADBANDS ARE A DODDLE TO MAKE AND ARE PERFECT FOR ADDING A LITTLE SPARKLE TO A SPECIAL EVENT. ALL YOU NEED IS SOME STRETCHY SEQUIN TRIM. ADD WHATEVER TAKES YOUR FANCY. WEAR SINGLY OR IN GROUPS FOR ADDED IMPACT.

YOU WILL NEED:

Stretchy sequin trim, found in most haberdashers
Scissors, needle, pins and thread
Clear glue
Clothes peg
In addition you might want to add:
  feathers, a brooch, a bow or
  anything else to make your
  headband stand out from the crowd!

1. Measure the amount of stretchy sequin trim you need by pulling it around your head to fit – allow a couple of centimetres for overlap.

2. Cut the trim and pin one end on top of the other, again making sure you have a couple of centimetres overlapping.

3. Try it on again, just to make sure it's right, then remove the pin and glue one of the ends on top of the other. This will stop your sequins coming undone and you'll get a good neat join that's not too bulky. Hold together with a clothes peg until completely dry.

4. Next sew the two ends together with a few small stitches for extra strength.

5. You can now trim as you wish – sewing or gluing the trim in place as desired over the join to hide it.

A couple of hints:

If you're trimming your headband with a bow, sew the bow together with a few small stitches first. This will stop it coming undone.

The cream headband is made by attaching each end of the stretchy trim to each end of an ornate central decoration. Glue each end in place first (this prevents the sequins coming undone), then when dry, sew each end in place too for strength, using small stitches. Finally glue a small circle of felt on top of each join for neatness. The exact look of the headband will depend on what you use.

Chapter two

HAT TRICKS REQUIRES YOU TO HAVE MASTERED SOME SLIGHTLY MORE FIDDLY TECHNIQUES, SUCH AS THE ABILITY TO HANDLE AND USE MILLINERY WIRE.

BEAUTIFUL BOW HEADPIECE

THIS LITTLE HEADPIECE WAS INSPIRED BY A VINTAGE FIND. THE ORIGINAL WAS MADE IN DEMURE SATIN FOR A '50S WEDDING AND SAT STRAIGHT ON TOP OF THE HEAD. I'VE GIVEN IT A MODERN TWIST, TRANSFORMING IT WITH EVENING FABRICS AND SETTING IT AT A JAUNTY ANGLE. I'VE MADE MY OWN BIAS BINDING OUT OF THE FABRIC I USED FOR THE BASE, BUT YOU CAN USE READY-MADE CONTRASTING BIAS BINDING IF YOU WISH. I'VE ALSO USED SOMETHING CALLED CRIN FOR THE TRIMMING, WHICH YOU CAN BUY FROM SPECIALIST SHOPS. THIS LITTLE NUMBER IS JUST BEGGING FOR ATTENTION!

YOU WILL NEED:

Bow pattern from page 172

Pins, scissors, pliers/wire cutters, needle,
  thread, thimble and measuring tape

Millinery buckram

Bondaweb

Millinery wire

Iron

Fabric remnant

Bias binding 2cm wide
  (I made my own for this hat
  – see Basic Techniques)

Crin (15cm wide)

Sequin trim for the centre
  (I used an elasticated type of trim)

Hat elastic

1. Photocopy the bow pattern from page 172. Cut out two in buckram, two in Bondaweb and two in fabric. Place the buckram bows on top of one another and hand-stitch the edges together.

2. Measure right round the edge of the bow and, with your pliers, cut a piece of millinery wire 8cm longer than your measurement to allow for overlap. Take care with the wire as it's springy and sharp.

3. Starting in the middle of the bow, use wire stitch (see Basic Techniques page 22) to attach the wire to the edge. Bend and shape the wire as you work your way around. Overlap the wire when you get to the end, laying the wires side by side. Stitch together to make sure the wire is really secure and won't budge.

4. Now iron your Bondaweb shapes to either side of your buckram shape, making sure you iron with the paper side uppermost. Now peel the paper off one side only and iron the fabric on to the bow until it sticks. Trim back all the excess fabric, peel back the paper from the other side of the bow and do the same thing again so that both sides are covered in fabric.

5. Measure enough bias binding to go around the edge of your bow remembering to include 2cm for an overlap. It's best to put the overlap in the middle where it will eventually be hidden by the sequin trim. Pin the bias binding in place (you'll have to put the pins in vertically as the buckram is tough), and stitch down, tacking in place first if you wish. (See Basic Techniques page 25 for help with sewing on bias binding.)

6. Now cut a piece of crin about 60cm long (you can make it longer or shorter if you wish) and remove the thread (if there is one) from the side. Fold so that the raw edges are in the middle and hold together with a few large straight stitches. It's quite springy. Now gather the middle together to form a bow, stitching again to hold in place.

7. Now put a pin in the front of your covered buckram shape as a reminder of which side is which and carefully shape your headpiece into a graceful curve, turning up the ends as shown.
Put the crin bow on to it at an angle, pin and sew in place going right through the buckram, using small secure straight stitches.

8. Cut a length of sequin trim (you want enough to wrap around the centre of your headpiece about three times). Put a dab of clear glue on the ends if needed to stop it fraying. Stitch in place with small stitches, making sure any overlap is at the back.

9. Attach your elastic in the places shown, stitching right through the buckram base following the guidelines in the Basic Techniques section (see page 29).
Add a tiny stitch to either side of the crin to hold your bow down.
Wear to the side at a jaunty angle.

I've discovered that crin is very slippery and rather dangerous on smooth floor surfaces. Don't leave bits lying on the floor as you might slip on it!

LITTLE LACE HALF-HAT

THE IDEA FOR THIS PRETTY MAKE-DO AND MEND HEADPIECE CAME ABOUT AFTER I FOUND A CUTE VINTAGE WEDDING CAP MADE OF MILLINERY NET AND LACE IN A SECOND-HAND SHOP. IT STRUCK ME THAT YOU COULD GET A SIMILAR EFFECT BY SLICING UP AN OLD STRAW HAT TO MAKE A BASE THEN BY STICKING OR SEWING A LACE-LIKE TRIM ON TOP. I BOUGHT A LENGTH OF FLOWERY COTTON TRIM, DYED IT WITH TEA TO GIVE IT A VINTAGE LOOK, STIFFENED IT WITH PVA AND THEN CUT IT UP TO MAKE SINGLE FLOWERS SO I COULD ATTACH THEM ALL INDIVIDUALLY. THE EFFECT YOU GET WILL DEPEND ON THE TYPE OF LACE TRIM YOU USE.

YOU WILL NEED:

Cotton lace-like trim that can be cut up to make individual
   flowers (the amount you'll need will depend on the size of
   hat you want to make, and the size of the flowers in the trim.
   I used 2m of trim)
Tea bag
PVA glue and a brush
Pins, scissors, chalk, needle and thread
An old straw-type hat in a pale colour
Bias binding (use a colour similar to your flowers 2 cm wide)
Tiny pearl-like beads
Hat elastic

1. Firstly dye your lace trim with tea to give it an aged look. Fill a small pan with boiling water, add a tea bag and dunk in your trim. Leave to soak for 5 minutes, then rinse briefly in cold water. Allow to dry then iron flat. Once the trim is dry, brush it with PVA glue to stiffen it. (I used my PVA undiluted to make the petals really stiff.) Allow to dry once again, then cut your trim into individual flower pieces and shape them slightly with your fingers to give them some movement.

2. Draw the shape of the base you want on to the crown of your old hat using the one in the picture as a guide. Cut out and tack all the way round, about 0.5cm from the edge. This will prevent the shape from stretching. Leave the tacking stitches in.

3. Next, pin your bias binding all the way around the edge of your base (over the tacking stitches) so that the raw edge of the base is sandwiched in the middle of the bias binding. Overlap the bias binding at the back by a couple of centimetres. Stitch down all the way round with a small neat running stitch going through all the layers. You don't need to use a special stitch for securing the bias binding on this occasion, as it won't be seen.

4. To stitch on your flowers, thread your needle with a double thread and put a knot on the end. Secure each flower centrally with a few small stitches before taking the thread to the back and moving on to the next flower. Start at the edges of the hat, and then move inwards to cover the whole crown, making sure the flowers overlap the bias binding and each other. You can sew six or seven flowers on with the same thread. Don't pull the thread too tight as you sew or the hat base will buckle.

5. Once all your flowers are in place, you can decorate further if you wish by sewing little pearl beads in the centre of each flower. Just go twice through each bead before moving on to the next one, sewing six or seven on with each thread. Keep the thread at the back taut but not too tight.

6. Finally attach the elastic to the hat to secure it following the guidelines in the Basic Techniques section (see page 29).

ORGANZA FLOWER COMBS

STYLISH VERSATILE HAIR ACCESSORIES
THAT CAN BE MADE IN MASSES
OF DIFFERENT COLOURS.

*this makes one comb, our model
opposite is wearing two*

YOU WILL NEED:

Six completed organza and
   wire flowers from the Flower
   Making Masterclass section
   (see page 34)
Clear glue
Pliers/wire cutters
Wool or floristry tape
Scissors, needle and thread
A hair comb
Small piece of ribbon
Clothes peg

1. First of all make up the flowers as instructed in the Flower Making Masterclass section (see page 34), making sure each flower has a stem of about 3.5cm. To create a cluster of three flowers, lay the first flower on top of the second as shown and bind together with a dab of glue and some thread. Do the same with the third flower. Repeat for the second set of three flowers.

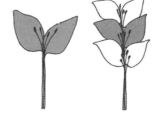

2. Using the pliers cut back the stems to about 2.5cm each. Once more, dab each stem with glue and bind together in the centre nice and tightly as shown. Neaten if desired by binding with wool or floristry tape. Bend the flowers into a slight arc.

3. Thread a needle with a double thread and put a knot on the end. Hold the flowers in place on the edge of the comb as shown. Stitch into the stem a couple of times to secure the thread and then wrap the flower on to the comb neatly by going around the prongs in order as far as you can in one direction, and then as far as you can in the other direction. Leave the needle dangling as you do this. Stitch into the stem a couple of times to finish and cut off the thread. You might have to do this twice or even three times as the flowers need to be really secure on the comb.

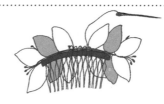

4. Finally make a small bow of ribbon and glue in place into the centre to cover any threads. Hold in place with a clothes peg to make sure it adheres really well.

5. Arrange the petals prettily, bending the ones at the back over to cover any threads so they don't show when the comb is in your hair.

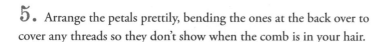

FABULOUS '50S PERCHER

YOU MIGHT NOT HAVE GUESSED, BUT THIS IS ANOTHER MAKE-DO AND MEND HAT FASHIONED OUT OF AN OLD STRAW NUMBER – ONE OF MY FAVOURITE TRICKS. I USED A RATHER UNFLATTERING '80S STYLE HAT, CHOPPED OFF THE TOP, AND USED THAT AS THE BASE FOR MY NEW FABULOUS '50S PERCHER. THE COLOUR OF THE HAT BASE WILL SHOW THROUGH THE LACE, SO TRY TO FIND SOMETHING YOU LIKE. I BOUGHT MY LOVELY ICE-CREAM COLOURED LACE TRIM AT A MARKET STALL WHERE IT WAS VERY CHEAP. I USED THREE DIFFERENT TYPES AND COLOURS OF LACE AND MIXED THEM ALL UP TO GIVE DIFFERENT SHADES. TRY TO FIND COTTON LACE TRIM WITH A BIT OF TEXTURE, AS IT WILL WORK BETTER THAN THE NYLON TYPE OF LACE. I'VE USED THREE SILK FLOWERS AS A FINAL FLOURISH. THEY'RE MADE USING THE METHOD FOR THE BONDAWEB FLOWERS IN THE FLOWER MAKING MASTERCLASS SECTION (SEE PAGE 38).

YOU WILL NEED:

An old straw hat with a rounded crown
Polystyrene head
Chalk
Tape measure, scissors, needle and thread
Millinery wire
Bias binding 2cm wide
Copydex glue and glue gun
5m of lace trim (it does depend a
  little on the size of your trim)
Three silk flowers to finish (see page 38)
Comb
Kirby grips

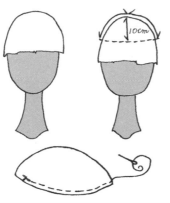

1. Cut off the brim of your old hat and place the crown on the polystyrene head. Use chalk to mark out the new hat base by measuring 10cm or so down from the centre point of the crown at the back, front and sides to get the right sort of size. The circumference of the new hat base should be in the region of 50cm – it's difficult to be precise as it will depend on your old hat and the size of your head. What you're aiming for is a little cap that will fit comfortably on the back of your head. Once you've drawn a line with the chalk, cut out the cap and sew a line of tacking stitches 0.5cm from the edge to stop it stretching.

2. Measure the circumference of your cap and cut off a piece of millinery wire 8cm longer to allow for overlap. Make a circle of the wire and attach using wire stitch to the outside of the cap (see Basic Techniques Section pages 22–23).

3. Next, pin your bias binding all the way around the edge of the cap (over the wire and the tacking stitches) so that the raw edge of the cap is sandwiched in the middle of the bias binding. Overlap the edges of the bias binding by a couple of centimetres.

4. Stitch down all the way round with a small neat running stitch going through all the layers. Mind the pins as you go and remove them one by one as you work. You don't need to use a special stitch to secure the bias binding here, as it won't be seen.

5. Next, put a thin layer of Copydex glue around the outside of the cap just above the bias binding and start sticking the lace on top, pressing firmly as you work your way around. Just work one row of lace. When you get back to where you started, cut the lace and stick it down neatly. Make sure the first row of lace covers the bias binding entirely, and overlaps the edge of the little cap.

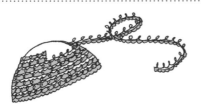

6. Now put a thin layer of glue just above the first row of lace, and stick down another row starting and finishing in the same place. Make sure the bottom of this row of lace overlaps the top of the last one. Each time you finish a row cut the lace and start again; this will help you mould the lace to the shape of the cap. Repeat. You can mix and mingle the types and colours of lace as you work. You'll find it much easier to stick the lace on to the cap by holding the cap in your hands rather than by putting it on the polystyrene head.

7. As you get to the very top of the cap you may have to cut your lace into small sections so that it lies flat. Put a small piece of lace in the centre to cover any gaps.

8. Now that the lace is done, check in the mirror and pin your flower trim into place. It's best to position it over the joins in the lace so that they're all covered up. Once you're happy you can glue gun your trim into position. Your hat is nearly finished.

9. Finally take a comb and position it at the front of your hat just above the edge. Positioning it here will mean you can wear the hat on the back of your head. Make sure the comb can't be seen when the hat is being worn.

10. Thread your needle with a double thread and put a knot on the end. Holding your comb in position in one hand, sew the comb on to the cap in two places, tying off the thread securely. Your comb should be able to move up and down a little.

11. You can now wear the hat by pushing the comb back into your hair. If you need extra stability, you can put hair-coloured kirby grips through the lace at the sides.

PRETTY PETALS

THIS FANTASTICAL HEADPIECE HAS A FEEL OF THE 1930S ABOUT IT AND WOULD BE LOVELY FOR A WEDDING OR SUMMER PARTY. IT'S MADE ON A HEADBAND SO IT'S VERY EASY TO WEAR – A GOOD OPTION FOR THOSE WHO ARE NERVOUS OF A HAT. IT INCORPORATES THE ROLLED THIN ELEGANT ORGANDY PETALS FROM THE FLOWER MAKING MASTERCLASS SECTION (SEE PAGE 40), SO ONCE YOU'VE GOT THE HANG OF THOSE, THIS HEADBAND IS FAIRLY STRAIGHT-FORWARD TO PUT TOGETHER. I USED WHITE COTTON ORGANDY FOR MY PETALS AND THEN DYED IT IN SMALL BATCHES TO GET A RANGE OF LOVELY COLOURS. I ALSO USED WHITE PETERSHAM RIBBON AND DYED THAT TOO – THE RIBBON IS USED TO COVER THE HEADBAND. DYEING THINGS YOURSELF GIVES A MORE VINTAGE LOOK, BUT IF YOU DON'T HAVE THE TIME THEN JUST SELECT PRETTY COLOURS. WASH NEW RIBBON BY HAND BEFORE USING TO SOFTEN IT UP READY FOR WRAPPING ROUND THE HEADBAND.

YOU WILL NEED:

0.5m–1m cotton organdy
  (depending on how many
  petals you want to make)
Floristry tape, thin wire, thread
Pliers/wire cutters
Clear glue
Scissors, pins, needle
2m petersham ribbon
  1.5cm wide
A narrow headband

1. Make up ten complete rolled thin elegant petals following the instructions in the Flower Making Masterclass (see page 40). In addition, make up six extra fan shaped section (b) pieces to use separately.

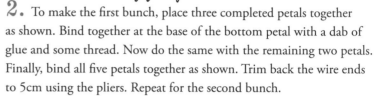

You're now going to make two bunches of five petals each.

2. To make the first bunch, place three completed petals together as shown. Bind together at the base of the bottom petal with a dab of glue and some thread. Now do the same with the remaining two petals. Finally, bind all five petals together as shown. Trim back the wire ends to 5cm using the pliers. Repeat for the second bunch.

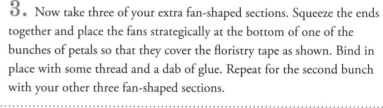

3. Now take three of your extra fan-shaped sections. Squeeze the ends together and place the fans strategically at the bottom of one of the bunches of petals so that they cover the floristry tape as shown. Bind in place with some thread and a dab of glue. Repeat for the second bunch with your other three fan-shaped sections.

4. Next cut two small pieces of petersham ribbon each 10cm long. Use a dab of clear glue to stick over each end of the headband, pressing the edges together at the bottom. Be careful with the glue and use it sparingly so it doesn't get everywhere.

5. Pin one bunch of petals 10cm from the end of your headband as shown with the petals facing downwards. Position the second bunch of petals 16cm from the other end of the headband. Remove the pins as you bind the petals into position using thread and glue. Press the wire ends as flat as you can against the headband using the pliers if need be.

6. Take your remaining long piece of petersham ribbon and put a dab of glue at one end. Press in place at one end of the headband (on the back) and start to wind the petersham up the headband overlapping each time. Go under the petals as far as you can and then wrap over the wire ends. There's no need for glue if you wrap nice and tightly.

7. Go all round the headband, cut off any excess petersham, and finish with a dab of glue (make sure you finish at the back of the headband).

MARIE ANTOINETTE

THIS IS A VERY VINTAGE-LOOKING HEADPIECE BASED ON THE CONCEPT OF A MILLINERY WIRE FRAME. THEY WERE WIDELY USED IN THE 1950S TO MAKE PRETTY LITTLE HALF-HATS. I'VE CALLED THIS THE MARIE ANTOINETTE BECAUSE OF ITS PASTEL COLOURS. I CAN JUST IMAGINE THE ELEGANT LADY DAINTILY SAVOURING SUGARED ALMONDS WHILST LOUNGING AROUND IN THIS. IT'S THE PERFECT EXCUSE FOR YOU TO DO JUST THE SAME! YOU'LL NEED TO GET YOUR HANDS ON SOME NARROW SATIN TUBING TO MAKE THIS. I CAN'T PRETEND IT'S EASY TO FIND, BUT THIS PROJECT IS WORTH INCLUDING JUST IN CASE YOU DO. THE TUBING HAS A STRING IN THE MIDDLE WHICH IDEALLY YOU SHOULD PULL OUT. ONCE THE STRING'S OUT OF THE WAY YOU'LL BE ABLE TO SLIP THE TUBING OVER THE MILLINERY WIRE. AGAIN, PLEASE DO BE CAREFUL WHEN USING MILLINERY WIRE. IT'S VERY SPRINGY, SO ALWAYS KEEP IT AWAY FROM YOUR EYES, AND ALWAYS USE PLIERS OR WIRE CUTTERS.

YOU WILL NEED:

1.75m strong millinery wire
Pliers or wire cutters
3m narrow satin tubing
Pins, tape measure, scissors, needle and thread
Clear glue
Narrow ribbon to trim
Hat elastic

1. Carefully measure and cut your 1.75m of wire then turn over the tips with the pliers to blunt them whilst you work. It's such a long bit of wire this is just an extra safety precaution. Now straighten the wire by working your way along the length bit by bit as shown bending it against the curve. It's tough wire so you need to have patience – and strength!

2. Cut a 1.8m length of the satin tubing and pull out the string inside. Prevent the tube's seam coming undone where you've cut it by putting in a few tiny stitches at the sides.

3. Carefully cut off one of the blunted ends of the wire (the wire will be too bulky to pass through the tube if you don't snip off the blunt end first) and push the wire through the tube, working your way along bit by bit until it's covered entirely. Ease back the fabric from the sharp end of the wire so you can get the pliers in and once again turn the tip over to make it safe. Fold a small piece of tube fabric over this end and glue it down as shown.

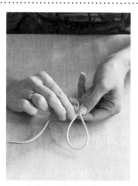

4. Now bend the wire as you see here to form a teardrop around 9-10cm long. Stitch through the fabric with small stitches where the wire touches and then bind the join with your thread to keep it secure.

5. Work your way along the wire bit by bit, creating the teardrop pattern as shown, stitching and binding each time. It's quite fiddly as you're working with a long length of stiff wire, but just do it section by section, pushing and pulling the wire as you go to wrestle it into shape. Try not to let the seam of the fabric tubing twist around as you work.

6. Once you've made ten teardrops you'll be nearing the end of your wire. As you start the final eleventh teardrop section take a look to see how much wire you need to complete it. Cut off any excess wire and fabric tubing. Before you stitch down the final piece of wire, ease back the fabric and bend over the tip of the wire again with your pliers. If you don't do this, it will poke through your fabric. Fold the spare bit of fabric back over the end of the wire and stick it down. Now you can stitch and bind the last piece into position.

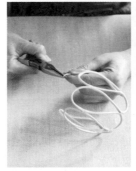

7. Use your hands to shape the headpiece into a soft curve as shown.

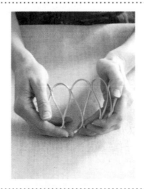

8. Make tiny bows from narrow ribbon and glue them on top of each join. Use a contrasting colour of ribbon or left-over tubing.

9. Cut a piece of hat elastic (mine is 54cm long but the length of yours will depend on your head size). Tie it into a loop as shown. Fold the elastic in half with the knot in the middle and sew each side halfway down each end of the headpiece, as shown. Sew over the elastic and into the fabric so the elastic can slide through the stitches. Secure your thread neatly.

Now go and eat sugared almonds like Marie Antoinette!

Chapter three

IN **MILLINERY MAGIC** I'VE INCLUDED SOME BASIC BLOCKED HATS AND A COUPLE OF HEADPIECES THAT WILL TEST YOUR HAND-SEWING AND MILLINERY SKILLS.

BUTTON HAT

THIS LITTLE DARLING IS ONE OF JUST A FEW
BLOCKED HAT PROJECTS IN THE BOOK. HOWEVER
IT'S NOT MADE ON A TRADITIONAL HAT BLOCK
BUT ON A LARGE VINTAGE DARNING MUSHROOM!
YOU CAN FIND THESE AT MARKETS, ON E-BAY, AND IN
ANTIQUES SHOPS. I'VE NOW GOT SEVERAL AND THEY
COST JUST A FEW POUNDS EACH SO THEY'RE MUCH
CHEAPER THAN 'PROPER' HAT BLOCKS.
IF YOU'RE NEW TO BLOCKING, THEN YOU'LL FIND
THESE DARNING MUSHROOMS EASY TO USE. IF
YOU'RE AN EXPERIENCED MILLINER, THEN TURN
YOUR HAND TO SOME MAKE-DO BLOCKING – IT'S
GREAT FUN! THE MUSHROOMS AREN'T ALL THE
SAME SIZE, BUT TRY TO FIND ONE THAT'S AT
LEAST 10CM IN DIAMETER – THAT WAY YOU'LL
GET A PROPER BUTTON-SHAPED HAT BASE.
I TRIMMED MY LITTLE HAT WITH A FLOWER
COMBINING VARIOUS TECHNIQUES FROM THE
FLOWER MAKING MASTERCLASS SECTION, BUT OF
COURSE FEEL FREE TO TRIM YOURS AS YOU WISH.
CAREFULLY READ THE SECTION ON BASIC
BLOCKING IN THE BASIC TECHNIQUES SECTION
(SEE PAGE 21) BEFORE ATTEMPTING THIS HAT AS
YOU MUST BE AWARE OF THE SAFETY ISSUES
WHEN USING STEAM AND BE FAMILIAR WITH THE
TECHNIQUE NEEDED FOR BLOCKING.

YOU WILL NEED:

Large vintage darning
   mushroom
Clingfilm
Wool felt hood – either a flare or
   capeline shape (unstiffened)
Pins, drawing pins, scissors,
   thimble, needle and thread
PVA glue diluted to the
   consistency of single cream,
   and a small brush
Hob top kettle
50cm narrow (1.5cm) petersham
   to tone with your hat
Hat elastic
Polystyrene display head
Strip of veiling 60cm x 15cm
   (make sure one of the 60cm
   veiling edges is the uncut,
   properly finished edge)
Iron

TO TRIM:

Flower of choice and glue gun to
   attach if desired
Pipe cleaners and pliers (to make
   spotted veiling)

TO MAKE THE BUTTON BASE:

1. Cover your darning mushroom top in clingfilm and unscrew the handle if possible as it gets in the way a bit at this stage.

2. Cut off the top portion of your felt hood (you need just enough to wrap round the darning mushroom) and if it's very floppy, brush the underside with diluted PVA solution. Allow to dry before steaming.

3. Thoroughly steam your felt and then pin and pull it into position over the top of the darning mushroom and round to the other side using the technique described in the Basic Blocking section in Basic Techniques (see page 21). Allow the felt to dry completely – overnight if necessary.

4. Remove the pins from the block and trim back the felt underneath to about 2cm from the edge.

5. Remove the felt carefully (if you screw back the darning mushroom handle at this stage it will help you get a good grip on the block). You might have to pull the felt a bit to remove it, but don't be afraid of stretching it a little, just pat it back into shape once it's removed. Make sure there's no clingfilm stuck to it.

6. Now neaten the trimmed edge (curved nail scissors can be quite useful for doing this) but don't chop off too much more felt.

7. Curve your petersham ribbon (see Basic Techniques section page 27) and sew in place round the trimmed edge of your hat 3 or 4mm in from the edge. Use stab stitch or slip stitch for a neat finish. Overlap the petersham at the back by a couple of centimetres and cut off any excess. This will now be the Centre Back (CB) of your hat. Place a pin in there to mark it.

8. Position your elastic and sew in place (see Attaching Hats with Elastic in the Basic Techniques section page 29). Now pop your hat on to a polystyrene display head so you can plan your veiling and trim.

TO TRIM THE HAT:

1. Take your strip of veiling and carefully press flat with the iron, if necessary. With the neat finished edge of the veiling closest to you, cut off the opposite top two corners as shown.

2. Thread your needle with a double thread and put a knot at the end. Gather up the veiling right the way along all the cut edges (don't gather the neat finished edge) as shown by going in and out of the little 'dots' that occur naturally in the veiling using a loose stitch.

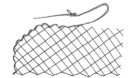

3. Once you get to the end, pull up the veiling to create a pleasing rounded shape. Secure and tie off the thread.

4. Pin the veiling in place around the Centre Front of your hat, positioning it so that it will come down a little in front of your eyes. The exact position will be up to you. Try the hat on to check that it works in the mirror, and once you're happy sew in place using small stab stitches going right the way through the hat.

5. Glue gun your chosen trim into place on top of the raw ends of the veiling so that it's all covered.

6. If you wish, you can make ultra-sophisticated spotted veiling using pipe cleaners. Use your pliers to cut little pieces of pipe cleaner about 1.5cm long. Bend one end over and then hook it around one of the little 'dots' in the veiling. Press the other end down with your fingers or pinch together with the pliers to hold in place.

SPARKLY MINI BERET

THIS LITTLE PARTY HAT IS BLOCKED IN THE SAME WAY AS
THE BUTTON HAT ON A VINTAGE DARNING MUSHROOM. THIS
TIME THOUGH, I'VE COVERED THE BASIC SHAPE IN SOME
SPARKLY SEQUIN FABRIC CUT FROM AN OLD TOP. YOU CAN
USE WHATEVER FABRIC YOU CHOOSE OF COURSE, BUT
SPARKLE CERTAINLY GIVES THIS HAT PERSONALITY! INSTEAD
OF USING FELT, I'VE USED MILLINERY BUCKRAM TO BLOCK
THIS HAT SHAPE, BUT FEEL FREE TO USE FELT IF YOU WISH.
BOTH BUCKRAM AND FELT CAN BE COVERED IN FABRIC, BUT IF
YOU USE FELT, IT MUST BE REALLY FIRM AND PRE-STIFFENED
AS IT NEEDS TO ACT AS A STRONG FOUNDATION FOR YOUR
FABRIC AND FOR THE BOW ON TOP. THE BOW'S FOUNDATION
SHOULD BE MADE OF UNSTIFFENED FELT.
  CAREFULLY READ THE SECTION ON BASIC BLOCKING IN
THE BASIC TECHNIQUES SECTION (SEE PAGE 21) BEFORE
ATTEMPTING THIS HAT AS YOU MUST BE AWARE OF THE
SAFETY ISSUES WHEN USING STEAM AND BE FAMILIAR
WITH THE TECHNIQUE NEEDED FOR BLOCKING.

YOU WILL NEED:

Large vintage darning mushroom

Clingfilm

Black felt hood – either a flare or capeline (buy one
  that's been pre-stiffened) or 50cm millinery buckram

Pins, drawing pins, scissors, thimble, needle and thread

Hob top kettle

Thin knitting needle

Fabric remnant for hat and bow

50cm of narrow (1.5cm) petersham ribbon to tone
  with your hat

Hat elastic

Polystyrene display head

Bow pattern from page 175

Small piece of millinery felt for the bow (use the
  left-over portion of the felt hood)

1.50m of sparkly textured trim for bow edge

Clear glue

Glue gun

TO MAKE THE BUTTON BASE:

1. Cover your darning mushroom in clingfilm and unscrew the handle if possible as it gets in the way a bit at this stage.

2. If you're using felt to make your hat, then cut off the top portion of your pre-stiffened felt hood and use this (you can use the rest of the felt to make trims). If you're using millinery buckram, cut two pieces large enough to cover your darning mushroom right round to the other side. Pin the buckram pieces together in the centre so they don't shift around when you're blocking them. You can also run your buckram under the tap to help soften it before you begin.

3. Thoroughly steam the felt or buckram and then pin and pull it into position over the top of the darning mushroom and round to the other side as shown, using the technique described in the Basic Blocking section in Basic Techniques (see page 21). Allow to dry completely – overnight if necessary.

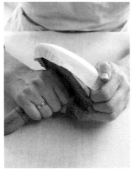

4. Remove the pins from the block and trim your foundation material back to about 2cm from the underside edge. Now carefully ease your foundation material off the block (if you screw the darning mushroom handle back on at this stage it will help you get a good grip on the block). You might have to pull a fair bit, especially if you use buckram (you could use a bit of steam to soften the back a little to help you remove it). If it's really stuck, use a thin knitting needle to help get between the block and the material. If the hat distorts whilst it's being removed, ease it back into shape with your hands. Make sure there's no clingfilm stuck to the underside of the hat.

5. Neaten the trimmed edge (curved nail scissors can be quite useful for doing this) but don't chop off too much more.

6. Take the fabric you wish to use to cover your hat and cut a piece large enough to go all the way round your little blocked hat shape with some to spare. Use the bias in the fabric to pull it neatly and tautly over the shape, pinning in place underneath as shown.

7. Thread a needle with double thread for strength and stitch the fabric down a couple of millimetres in from the underside edge. Use a small tacking stitch to do this. When you're done, trim back the fabric so that it's nice and neat. If you're using sequin fabric then don't trim it right back but leave a little spare so that you can stick it back underneath the edge with some clear glue to stop the threads and sequins working loose.

8. Curve your petersham ribbon (see Basic Techniques section page 27) and sew in place round the edge of your hat 3 or 4mm in from the edge. Use stab stitch or slip stitch for a neat finish. Overlap the petersham at the back by a couple of centimetres and cut off any excess. This will now be the Centre Back (CB) of your hat. Mark it with a pin.

9. Position your elastic and sew in place (see Attaching Hats with Elastic in the Basic Techniques section page 29). Now pop your hat on to a polystyrene display head.

TO MAKE YOUR COVERED BOW TRIM:

1. Photocopy and cut out the bow pattern from the back of the book (page 175). Press your millinery felt flat and pin the pattern in place on top. Cut out. This will act as your foundation. Remove pins and pattern.

2. Now fold your fabric with right sides together. Pin the bow pattern in place on top and cut out. This will give you two fabric pieces with which to cover your bow.

3. Cover each side of the bow in turn with the fabric pieces by laying each piece on top of the felt with right side up, pinning in place and tacking down round the edges.

4. Take your trim and sew in place around the edge, starting in the middle of the short side of the bow. Try to make your stitches as small as possible on the trim side so that you don't notice them, and use a matching thread. When you get back round to the start, cut the trim off flush and use a tiny dab of clear glue to hold it in position.

5. Now turn the bow over and sew the trim in place on the other side too, matching it up so it's even. You'll have to stitch right through to the other side of the bow and the trim, but again, keep your stitches as small as possible and you really won't notice them especially if you use a textured trim. When you get back round to the start, cut the trim off flush and use a tiny dab of clear glue to hold it securely in position.

6. Finally use a small running stitch to sew the edges of the trim together so that you don't see the felt sandwiched inside.

7. Pinch the bow together in the middle and, using a double thread for strength, sew right through the centre of the bow to create the shape you see here. The millinery felt is quite tough, so you might need a thimble to do this. Make sure you tie off your thread really securely.

8. If the fabric buckles away from the bow in its new pinched position, then use tiny stab stitches to keep it in place.

9. Finally pin the bow in position on your hat, check in the mirror that you're happy, and then glue gun or sew into position securely.

EXTRA TIP:
You can line your hat by sticking a large circle of felt inside, if you wish.

SUMMER FELT HAT

THIS BEAUTIFUL PIECE ENABLES YOU TO HAVE A GO AT BLOCKING WITHOUT HAVING TO INVEST IN PRICEY EQUIPMENT OR MASTER TRICKY TECHNIQUES. TO FORM THE CROWN, ALL YOU NEED IS A POLYSTYRENE DISPLAY HEAD, WHILST THE BRIM IS CUT OUT FLAT IN THREE SECTIONS AND SEWN INTO PLACE BY HAND. I'VE MADE THIS HAT IN MILLINERY FELT, WHICH IS ONE OF THE EASIEST MATERIALS FOR AMATEURS TO USE AS IT'S SO FORGIVING. PEOPLE OFTEN THINK FELT IS ONLY SUITABLE FOR WINTER HATS, BUT IN A LIGHT COLOUR AND TEAMED WITH LACE I THINK IT MAKES A PERFECT SUMMER HAT AS YOU CAN SEE HERE. IF YOU WANT A REALLY SIMPLE PROJECT THEN JUST LEAVE OUT THE LACE, YOU'LL STILL HAVE A BEAUTIFULLY ELEGANT VINTAGE-STYLE HAT.
  CAREFULLY READ THE SECTION ON BASIC BLOCKING IN THE BASIC TECHNIQUES SECTION (SEE PAGE 21) BEFORE ATTEMPTING THIS HAT AS YOU MUST BE AWARE OF THE SAFETY ISSUES WHEN USING STEAM AND BE FAMILIAR WITH THE TECHNIQUE NEEDED FOR BLOCKING.

You will need to use normal pins to block this hat as drawing pins are too short and will pop out of the polystyrene head.

YOU WILL NEED:

Hob top kettle

Clingfilm

Polystyrene display head

Wool felt hood – either a flare or capeline shape (unstiffened)

Pins, scissors, chalk, thimble, needle and thread

Iron

Pressing cloth

The brim and bow patterns from the back of the book (see pages 174–5)

Small amount of lace fabric

Sewing machine

Pinking shears

Measuring tape

Hat elastic

1. Heat up the water in your hob top kettle until there's a good head of steam. Place some clingfilm over your polystyrene head to protect it.

2. Carefully hold the crown section of your felt hood in the steam to soften it. Be extra vigilant and keep the ends of the hood away from the gas flame or electric ring. Then pull the hood over the polystyrene head with both hands. Using the blocking method described in the introduction (see page 21), pin the felt in position around the head just above the eyes and ears. Make sure the blocked felt is as smooth as possible.

3. Whilst the top part of the hood (the crown of the hat) is drying on the head, chop off the bottom two thirds and press it out flat using an iron. Be careful your iron doesn't get too hot, and use a cloth between the iron and the felt to stop it burning.

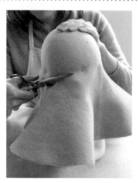

4. Photocopy the brim and bow patterns (see pages 174–5), then cut out three identical brim pieces in felt and three in lace, making sure you always place the pattern on the right side of the felt or fabric. Cut one bow piece in felt and one in lace.

5. Now place each lace piece on top of a felt piece (wrong side of lace on right side of felt) and using a straight stitch on your machine (use a slightly longer stitch length than normal), sew around each piece about 1cm in from the edge. Now trim back each piece with the pinking shears about 0.5cm in from the edge, to create a decorative zigzag edge.

6. Once the crown of your hat is completely dry, place a pin in the centre and measure 12cm down from this point at the front, back, and sides, marking with chalk. Join up the points with a nice smooth even line going all the way around to create a little skullcap. Cut out the cap with your normal scissors.

7. Stitch around the edge of the cap 1cm in, using the straight stitch on your machine. This will prevent the cap from stretching. Then use pinking shears to create a decorative zigzag finish between the cut edge and the stitching.

8. Now firmly pin the cap back on to the polystyrene head marking the Centre Front (CF) and Centre Back (CB) with chalk.

9. Pin the first of your brim pieces to the cap with the left point about 10cm from the Centre Back, pulling it fairly tautly around the cap. The brim piece should be positioned about 1cm from the edge of the cap. Ease off the head and sew in position by hand using stab stitches.

10. Place the cap back on the head and pin the second brim piece in position overlapping the first as shown and slanting upwards so that it's about 3cm from the edge at the furthest point on the right. Again pull fairly taut. Remove from the head and again stab stitch into position. You might need a thimble at this point as the layers get quite thick.

11. Repeat with the third brim piece, this time sloping it further up the cap until it's about 5cm from the edge. Turn the last few centimetres of the brim piece back on itself as shown. Pin firmly in place and once more remove from the head and stab stitch into position, concealing the stitches as much as possible.

12. Take the bow that you made earlier, pinch together in the middle and, using a double thread, sew through the folds to hold the bow in position.

13. Find the most flattering position for your bow (look in the mirror with the hat on to do this) then put the hat back on the polystyrene head. Pin the bow into place and using a double thread for strength, stitch into position, going right through all the layers, using tiny stab stitches wherever possible.

14. That's your hat done. If you wish you can put in tiny stitches to hold the three brim pieces together where they overlap. I also used a couple of invisible stitches to hold the lace in position on the turned-up edge of the brim so the lace didn't gape.

15. Now measure the elastic to fit your hat and attach according to the instructions in The Basic Techniques section (see page 29).

SIMPLE FELT CLOCHE *(with a fancy trim)*

I'VE DESIGNED THIS PROJECT TO GIVE YOU A BASIC INTRODUCTION TO BLOCKING A SIMPLE FITTED FELT HAT ON A TRADITIONAL HAT BLOCK. MAKE SURE YOU READ THE GUIDE TO STEAMING AND BLOCKING IN THE BASIC TECHNIQUES SECTION FIRST AS IT'S IMPORTANT YOU KNOW HOW TO STEAM SAFELY (SEE PAGE 21). TO MAKE THIS HAT YOU'LL NEED A BASIC DOMED HAT BLOCK IN YOUR HEAD SIZE PLUS A WOODEN BREADBOARD. IT'S NOT VERY CONVENTIONAL – BUT IT WORKS! YOU'LL ALSO NEED A STAND FOR YOUR BLOCK BUT YOU CAN ALWAYS IMPROVISE WITH A MUG OR SOMETHING SIMILAR. TRY TO FIND SOMETHING ABOUT 10CM HIGH.

YOU CAN EITHER LEAVE THIS HAT UN-STIFFENED TO MAKE IT COMPLETELY SQUASHY, OR ALTERNATIVELY YOU CAN STIFFEN THE TOP WITH A LITTLE PVA SOLUTION TO GIVE IT A BIT MORE STRUCTURE.

The trim is made of stiffened fabric circles. Fancy that!

YOU WILL NEED:

A wool felt hood – flare shape (un-stiffened)

PVA glue diluted to the consistency of single cream (you can use this solution for the hat and for the trim) and a small brush

Hob top kettle

A domed hat block in your head size

Clingfilm

A stand for your block or a mug or jar about 10cm high to place the block on

A thin wooden breadboard/chopping board

Drawing pins

Steam iron

A piece of strong ribbon to wrap round the block as you're blocking

Scissors, pins, thimble, needle and thread, chalk, measuring tape

Sewing machine

Petersham ribbon for headband inside the hat either 1.5 or 2.5cm wide

Old toothbrush

Fine sandpaper

Blu-Tack (or similar)

TO TRIM:

Scraps of fabric

Paper

Pinking shears

Brooch

TO MAKE YOUR HAT:

1. If you want to stiffen the felt flare a little then brush the top of the inside with your PVA solution and allow it to dry before you begin.

2. Clear your work surface and get a good head of steam going in your kettle. Cover your block with clingfilm and put it on your stand if you have one, or on your mug if you don't (for the mug use Blu-Tack to hold it to the block). Place in the middle of your wooden breadboard.

3. Steam the felt hood really thoroughly as shown – be careful, as the steam can escape from open areas of the hood in unexpected places and make sure that your hood doesn't come into contact with the flame or electric ring on your cooker. Don't just steam in one area but change the position of the hood as you go so that you spread the steam evenly. You need to steam until you see little beads of perspiration appearing on the outside of the felt.

4. Once the felt is really soft, quickly and firmly pull the hood over your block and drawing-pin the back of it directly on to the breadboard underneath the block. Now pin the front a few centimetres out from the block on to the board as you can see here. Do the same with both of the sides. If you need the felt to become more supple in order for it to reach the breadboard then carefully pick the breadboard up with one hand, steadying the block and stand with your other, and direct steam at the sides. If it's too heavy or awkward for you to do this then leave the block where it is and use a good blast of steam from your steam iron instead.

5. Take your strong ribbon and wrap it firmly round the base of the block, pinning it at the back. If the pins pop out from around the sides of the felt when you do this, then put more pins in so it's anchored firmly in place.

6. Pin the sides out a little more and then leave the blocked felt to dry thoroughly. When dry, remove the ribbon. Don't worry if it's left a mark. See Extra Tips on page 118.

7. Now to measure out your hat. Put a pin in the centre of the crown then measure 18cm down the back, 26cm to the front and 23cm on each side. I've designed this hat to be cut up a little at the back so it doesn't catch on your collar. Mark with chalk and then join the marks together to create a hat shape. Make sure the sides are nice and even. Remove all the drawing pins and take the hat off the block.

8. Now carefully cut out the hat along the line you've drawn. Try to use long cutting movements with the scissors to keep the edge as smooth as possible. See Extra Tips for hints on achieving a smooth edge. Try the hat on for size and adjust as needed, trimming back the felt to suit.

9. Machine stitch with a straight stitch (use a slightly longer stitch length than normal) around the edge of the hat as shown. This will give a neat finish and will also stop the edge stretching.

10. Now you're going to attach a fitted petersham headband. This will stop the hat from stretching when worn and ensure the correct fit. To make the fitted headband refer to the Basic Techniques section (see page 27). When you come to stitch the headband in place inside the hat, use slip stitch, but make sure your stitches don't go all the way through to the right side of your felt hat. You want to 'bury' the stitches inside the felt so they don't show.

NOW YOU ARE READY TO TRIM YOUR HAT:

1. To make the circle trim, stiffen some scraps of fabric with PVA solution (put the fabric on an old plastic bag to do this). I used scraps of lace and linen to give a variety of textures. Hang up to dry.

2. Make a paper template (mine was 7.5cm in diameter) and use it to cut out 24 stiffened fabric circles with pinking shears. These give a nice decorative edge. Place your hat on the block and then fold each circle in half and pin the fold on to your hat starting at the Centre Front (CF) as shown, making sure all the circles overlap each other. You want 12 circles evenly spaced on either side. Make sure the circles also overlap the edge of the felt hat a little to give a soft look.

3. Once all the folded circles are pinned in position, take the hat off the block and sew where you've pinned, using stab stitches at the back and a couple of larger stitches at the front. Sew down four or five circles at one go, using a double thread. Use a thread that matches the trimming. Colour any threads that show on the back of the hat with a marker pen to match the felt.

4. Remove all the pins and finish with a pretty brooch.

EXTRA TIPS:

To remove any ribbon marks left from the blocking process, steam the bristles on an old toothbrush and with the hat on the block, brush the pile of the felt back up.

To even out the edges of felt hats you can use a small piece of fine sandpaper.

PLEATED PETERSHAM HEADBAND

THIS HEADBAND IS A DELIGHT TO WEAR
AND ALWAYS ELICITS APPRECIATIVE
REMARKS FROM THE ASSEMBLED
CROWDS. IT WOULD BE LOVELY FOR A
WEDDING, LOOKING STUNNING ON EITHER
THE BRIDE OR ONE OF HER GUESTS. IT'S
NOT HARD TO MAKE, BUT THE VINTAGE
TECHNIQUE USED TO PLEAT THE RIBBON
DOES TAKE SOME PRACTICE AND
PATIENCE. I DYED THE RIBBON MYSELF
TO GIVE IT A REALLY FADED VINTAGE
FEEL, BUT YOU DON'T NEED TO DO THIS
– JUST CHOOSE A PRETTY COLOUR. I'VE
INCLUDED A VEIL IN THIS HEADPIECE, BUT
YOU COULD EASILY OMIT IT IF YOU PREFER
TO WEAR YOUR HEADBAND EVERY DAY.

YOU WILL NEED:

4m petersham ribbon 2.5cm wide

Measuring tape

Needle and thread, scissors, thimble

Strip of veiling 46cm x 16cm (make sure one
of the 46cm veiling edges is the uncut,
properly finished edge)

Small piece of petersham ribbon 1.5cm wide
for the central bow

Fabric-covered headband

Pins

Polystyrene head

Glue gun

Thin craft felt

Hole punch

Clear glue

Iron

HOW TO PLEAT THE PETERSHAM:

You'll need 1m of petersham ribbon for each little roundel, and you need to make four roundels in total for this headband.

1. Thread your needle with a long single thread the length of your arm and put a knot at the end. Hold the 1m length of petersham in front of you and make a small pleat of about 1cm at the top. Push the pleat slightly to the side and hold it in place at the corner with a tiny stitch (make sure your knot is at the back of course). If you don't push the pleat to the side, it won't look right. Leave the needle dangling. Now make another pleat in the same way and fold it half-way up on top of the first and once again push slightly to the side. Pick up your needle and hold the pleat in place at the corner with another tiny stitch.

2. Continue like this down the length of the ribbon, being careful not to let your pleats get bigger as you work. Your thread should last you until you reach the end.

Once you're reached the bottom of the ribbon, secure and tie off your thread. (The right-hand picture shows you what the back of the ribbon will look like.)

3. Now thread your needle again, this time with a knotted double thread, and pick up the ribbon. On the opposite side to the edge you've just pleated, catch the very tips of ribbon on your needle so that they all end up on your thread.

4. When you get to the end, pull the pleated ribbon up on the thread and it will start to curve.

Pull until the pleated ribbon looks like the picture. Secure and cut off your thread.

Shape your ribbon as shown, tucking in the raw ends and holding it together with a couple of tiny stitches.

TO ASSEMBLE
THE HEADBAND:

1. Take your strip of veiling and carefully press flat with an iron if necessary. Cut off the top two corners opposite the neat finished edge of the veiling. Thread your needle with a double thread and put a knot at the end. Gather up the veiling right the way along all the cut edges (don't gather the neat finished edge) as shown, by sewing in and out of the little 'dots' that occur naturally in the veiling. Once you get to the end pull up the veiling to a length of about 26cm, pushing the bulk of the gathers to the two outside edges.

2. Don't tie off your thread yet in case you need to make adjustments, but pin the veiling centrally on to the top of the headband as shown. (Do this on your polystyrene head if it helps.)
Once you're happy with the look, tie off your thread, and sew your veiling securely on to the top of the fabric-covered headband.

3. Now find the centre of the headband and mark it with a pin. Glue the first two roundels to either side of this central point using the glue gun. Then glue the second two roundels into position. The roundels should cover up the raw edges of the veiling. Make a small bow and glue to the centre.

4. Finally, decorate your veiling by punching out small spots of craft felt using a hole punch. You may have to trim them to get them looking really precise. Glue each one using a tiny dab of clear glue to the 'dots' around the edge of the veiling.

ASCOT WORTHY WINNER

WOW – WHAT A HAT! EASY TO WEAR AS IT'S ON A HEADBAND, AND NOT TOO DIFFICULT TO MAKE EITHER, THIS IS A REAL SHOWSTOPPER. YOU CAN EITHER MAKE A SMALL VERSION (LIKE THE BLACK AND WHITE ONE) OR BE BRAVE AND MAKE A LARGER ONE. THE WHOLE CONCEPT IS BASED ON CIRCLES MADE OF MILLINERY WIRE. CHECK OUT THE BASIC TECHNIQUES SECTION TO SEE HOW TO MAKE THESE. THE EXACT LOOK OF THE HAT WILL DEPEND ON THE FABRICS YOU USE: THINNER SILKY FABRICS GIVE MORE DEFINITION; THICKER FABRICS, LIKE THE WHITE FABRIC OVERLEAF, WILL LOOK MORE PUFFED.

YOU WILL NEED:

Firm millinery wire

Measuring tape

Pliers/wire cutters

Scissors, pins, needle and thread

Fabric remnants

Fabric-covered headband

Polystyrene head

Clear glue

Trim of your choice, feathers, or cover button
  (the type you can cover in fabric)

Scrap of craft felt and pinking shears

TO MAKE THE SMALL VERSION:

1. First make two wire circles following the instructions in The Basic Techniques section (see pages 22–23). You can make them any size you like (mine were about 45cm and 55cm in circumference, plus an additional 8cm overlap for joining the wire). Make sure the joins in your wire are really secure.

2. Now lay your first wire circle down on the wrong side of your chosen fabric and cut out a circle of fabric big enough to wrap it in. You can get an idea of how much you'll need by scrunching the fabric up into the centre. You'll need enough fabric to come right back into the centre of the circle fairly tautly once it's gathered up.

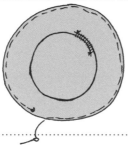

3. Using a double thread, put a knot on the end, secure the thread in the fabric and work a running stitch around the circle about 0.5cm in from the edge.

4. Put the wire circle back inside the fabric circle and pull up the gathers so the wire is completely enclosed in the fabric. The fabric should feel taut around the wire as previously mentioned.

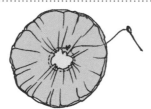

5. Stitch into the gathers further to make sure they're really secure and tie off the thread. Repeat for the second circle.

6. Now pin the small circle on top of the larger one in the centre with both sets of gathers facing upwards. Stitch together in the centre in a small circle with a double thread using small stab stitches. You can now give some shape to the wire circles by bending them slightly in whatever way you choose.

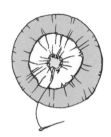

7. Now put your headband on a polystyrene head and pin the circles on to the side, pinning through the centre and through the fabric of the headband. This stage is tricky.

8. Try it on, and once you're happy that the circles are in a flattering position, you can sew the circles on to the headband. Don't worry about messy sewing at the back or stitching over the headband as you'll cover this with a piece of craft felt. The main thing is that the circles are good and firm and can't move around.

9. Trim as desired covering the central gathers with whatever you choose. If you wish you can sew on a cover button (as in the large version of the hat, page 128). I trimmed my little one with a pretty vintage floral trim that I found in a market.

10. Finally cut out a small circle of craft felt using pinking shears and glue in place on the back right over the headband to cover any messy sewing.

TO MAKE THE LARGER VERSION:

1. Make up your wire circles as before but add either one or two slightly larger ones. I wouldn't get any bigger than about 70cm circumference or the hat will be hard to handle and stabilise.

2. Sew together your two largest circles first, as before, with gathers all facing up. You can now shape the wires.

3. Now pin these circles on to your headband as before – it's quite fiddly and harder with larger circles, but it can be done!

4. When you're happy with the look, sew these on to the headband as firmly as possible. Do remember, with a larger hat you need to balance the weight carefully so it doesn't slip to one side. The easiest way to do this is to keep trying the hat on and adjusting the circles and the way they're shaped until the balance is right. Don't attach your circles too far over to one side.

5. Now shape any remaining circles and sew these on top of the ones you've already attached one at a time.

6. Finally you can trim your hat by slipping feathers between the layers and sewing or gluing them in place as near to the centre as possible so you don't distort your hat elsewhere. Do remember once again to balance the weight of any trim – you don't want your hat slipping off!

7. Finish with craft felt on the back as before.

EXTRA TIPS:

A frou-frou feather will give this hat show-stopping appeal.

Be careful to balance the weight of the hat. Don't fix your circles too far to one side.

Use fabric to match your outfit for a co-ordinated look.

THE MINI TOP HAT

EVERY TIME I RUN A HAT-MAKING WORKSHOP I'M ASKED TO SHOW PEOPLE HOW TO MAKE A MINI TOP HAT FROM SCRATCH. IT'S A SHAPE THAT'S INCREDIBLY POPULAR WITH BRIDES AND BURLESQUE BEAUTIES, COMBINING AS IT DOES BOTH CLASSIC STYLE CREDENTIALS AND CHEEKY FLIRTATION. HOWEVER, MAKING THIS DOES REQUIRE A CERTAIN AMOUNT OF SKILL AND PATIENCE AND INVOLVES SOME TOP OF THE RANGE COUTURE MILLINERY METHODS. IT'S NOT FOR BEGINNERS, BUT I'VE DONE MY BEST TO SIMPLIFY THE TRADITIONAL CONSTRUCTION TECHNIQUES SO THAT THOSE WHO ENJOY A CHALLENGE CAN GIVE IT A GO AT HOME.
  I'VE MADE THIS TOP HAT WITH BOTH STRETCHY AND NON-STRETCHY FABRIC AND HAVE FOUND THAT STRETCHY FABRIC IS EASIER TO WORK WITH. I THINK THE STRETCHY GLITTERY FABRIC I'VE USED HERE IS PERFECT. IT DOES MEAN THOUGH THAT YOU MUST USE A LOWER IRON SETTING – AND TAKE EXTRA CARE WHEN YOU ADHERE THE FABRIC TO THE BONDAWEB. USE A PRESSING CLOTH IF NEED BE.

YOU WILL NEED:

0.5m millinery buckram

Needle, strong thread, thimble,

Copydex glue, scissors, pins,
  tape measure, iron, pliers/wire
  cutters, chalk

Glue gun

400g tin of tomatoes to act as
  a block

Hob top kettle

Firm millinery wire

Bondaweb

0.5m fabric (you'll use less
  but cutting on the bias
  means you'll need a bit more
  than usual)

Bias binding (2cm wide) and
  enough to go round the
  brim edge

Small piece of petersham
  (1.5cm wide) ribbon to go
  inside your top hat to finish
  it off

Trim of choice (I used a large
  handmade flower)

TO MAKE THE CROWN:

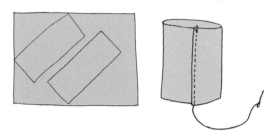

1. First cut out two pieces of buckram on the bias 11cm x 25cm. Place one on top of the other, then wrap them around the can of tomatoes so the short edges overlap. Mark the overlap with chalk. Take the buckram off the can, pin together and sew in place really firmly using small straight stitches and double thread. Take out the pins and you'll now have a buckram tube.

2. Get a good head of steam going on your kettle following the safety advice given in Basic Techniques (see page 20). Put the top and bottom ends of the tube into the steam one at a time and then use your fingers to pull the ends out wider. You want to give the tube a good top hat shape. Only use the steam on the edges of the tube, as you don't want to distort the shape elsewhere. Try not to get dents in the buckram but keep it smooth as you work.

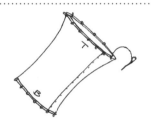

3. Measure around each end of the tube in turn and cut two pieces of millinery wire to fit with a 6cm overlap. Join the wire to make two circles following the technique in the Basic Techniques section (see page 23). Sew each circle of wire to the correct ends of the tube using wire stitch (see page 22). Decide on a top and a bottom and mark with a T and a B so that you remember which is which.

4. Now place the top of your tube (T) down on to some flat buckram. Draw around it with chalk and cut out the circle. Cut out a circle of Bondaweb exactly the same size, and a circle of fabric 1.5cm bigger all round. Iron the Bondaweb on to your buckram circle, paper-side up, peel off the paper and then iron this on to the wrong side of your fabric bang in the centre. (If you're using thin fabric you might need to iron two layers of Bondaweb on to your buckram to stop the buckram texture showing through your fabric.)

5. Snip through the fabric up to the buckram circle to create tabs, place on top of your tube and glue the fabric tabs to the outside. Allow to dry.

6. Now cut out a strip of fabric on the bias 6cm wider and 3cm longer than your tube (if you're using stretch fabric, you don't need to worry about the bias). Fold over the top edge of the fabric by 1cm so it's nice and neat, and press.

7. Line up this pressed edge with the top of your tube and pin the corner in place. Pin the opposite bottom corner in place at the bottom of the tube and then pull the fabric around the tube, pinning it in place along the top edge as you go, using the bias or stretch to help get a good, curved shape. Keep the fabric taut. When you get back round to where you started the fabric ends will overlap, so fold the upper edge of the fabric under to neaten and pin it in place.

8. Remove the pin from the bottom edge of the fabric and tuck the fabric under itself all the way round so that the folded edge of the fabric is in line with the bottom edge of the tube. Don't tuck the fabric underneath the tube because as this top hat is unlined you want the inside to look as neat as possible when you've finished. (If there's a lot of fabric, trim it back a little.) You'll have to go round the tube a couple of times to get the fabric as smooth, neat and taut as possible. Pin in place along the edge.

9. Slip stitch the top edge in place with tiny neat stitches, taking out the pins as you go. Adjust the fabric again to make sure it's smooth, then use little stab stitches to secure the fabric at the bottom of the tube going right through it.

10. Finally slip stitch or stab stitch the side seam together where the fabric overlaps and remove all pins. That's your crown made.

NOW TO MAKE YOUR BRIM:

1. Place the bottom of your crown on to your buckram and draw a circle 3.5cm larger all round with chalk. Cut it out then cut out two Bondaweb circles and two fabric circles exactly the same size.

2. Measure round the edge of the buckram circle and cut a piece of millinery wire to this length plus 8cm for overlap. Join the wire to make a circle as directed in the Basic Techniques section (see page 23) and sew the circle of wire to the underside of your brim circle using wire stitch.

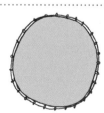

3. Iron the Bondaweb (paper-side up) on to each side of the buckram and, one side at a time, peel back the paper and iron the fabric into place too. Again, if you're using thin fabric you might need to use two layers of Bondaweb on top of the buckram to stop the buckram texture showing through your fabric. Trim off any little excess bits of fabric.

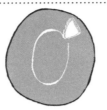

4. Take your crown again and squeeze to create a slightly oval shape. (Make sure your seam is to the side so that it will eventually be covered by whatever trim you use.) Place this oval crown on top of your brim and draw around it with chalk.

5. Now push your scissors into the middle of the brim and cut around and up to within about 1.5cm of the line you've just drawn.

6. Carefully cut snips up to within 2mm of this line to create tabs. Don't actually go up to the line, as you won't get the right fit when you come to put the brim and the crown together.

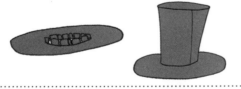

7. Fold back the tabs and sparingly glue their outer edges. Let the glue go tacky then stick to the inside of the crown. It's really important you let the glue go tacky so that it doesn't seep through your fabric. Leave it to dry.

8. Now bend the wire up at the sides of the brim to create a proper top hat shape.

TO FINISH:

1. Take your bias binding and measure how much you need to go around the edge of your brim, leaving 2cm for an overlap. Fold in half lengthways and tack to the edge of your brim, making sure the overlap matches up with the seam in your crown at the side. This way, you can get your trim to hide this overlap too as well as the seam when you position it. Stab stitch the bias binding in place going right through the brim to catch each side of the bias binding (see Basic Techniques page 25).

2. Attach elastic to your top hat as explained in Basic Techniques (see page 29). Now curve a little piece of petersham ribbon (see page 27) and stick it to the inside edge of your top hat to neaten it off.

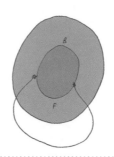

3. Trim your top hat as desired, perhaps using a flower from the Flower Making Masterclass section. Use a glue gun to stick your trim to the top hat – remembering to place it over the seams and joins to hide them.

Chapter four

THE **CUT & SEW COLLECTION** IS FOR THOSE OF YOU WHO ARE CONFIDENT USING A SEWING MACHINE. I'LL SHOW YOU HOW TO MAKE BASIC PATTERNS THAT YOU CAN ADAPT TO SUIT YOUR OWN STYLE AND HEAD SIZE.

CUT & SEW COLLECTION INTRODUCTION

I THOUGHT IT WOULD BE FUN TO INCLUDE SOME FABRIC HATS IN THE BOOK. IF YOU'RE REASONABLY GOOD AT USING A SEWING MACHINE, THEN YOU WON'T FIND THESE TOO HARD. CERTAIN HAND SEWING SKILLS ARE ALSO USED IN THE CONSTRUCTION OF THESE HATS. THESE ARE OUTLINED IN BASIC TECHNIQUES AT THE START OF THE BOOK. INSTEAD OF PROVIDING PATTERNS, I'VE OPTED TO SHOW YOU HOW TO MAKE YOUR OWN INDIVIDUAL TEMPLATE SO THAT THESE HATS WILL FIT NO MATTER WHAT YOUR HEAD SIZE. IT ALSO MEANS THAT YOU CAN ALTER THE SIZE OF THE BRIM OR THE HAT HEIGHT OR WHATEVER ELSE YOU FANCY.

Here are a few tips before you begin:

✳ A domestic sewing machine is fine for all these projects, but do bear in mind that occasionally you'll need to sew through three or four thick layers, so go carefully.

✳ Hatmaking often involves sewing circular shapes on to straight shapes. I've found through experience that there's no 'best way' to do this – you just have to go slowly and watch for snags and gathers underneath the foot of the machine. Cutting tabs into curved edges on completion will help the hats look smoother.

✳ I usually sew over my pins – but remember to do so with care.

✳ Using the bias in fabric helps create much smoother shapes and gives fabric a bit of natural stretch. Please use the bias where it's recommended.

✳ When it comes to making the patterns, either use newspaper or buy yourself a roll of cheap paper. The type used for children's drawing is great as you can write on it and there's no newsprint to rub off on your fabrics. It lasts a long time too.

✳ When giving instructions for making patterns, I'll use the words 'circumference', 'radius' and 'diameter' – so do check you understand these terms. You'll also see I use the number 6.28 quite a lot. For experts this is 2 x pi, and if you divide the circumference of a circle by this number you'll get the radius. This is handy for making hat patterns.

✳ You'll need a compass so that you can draw circles. If the circle you want is too big for your compass then tie two pencils to a piece of string (measure the string to be the length you need). Hold one pencil still in the centre whilst you use the other pencil to draw your circle, pulling the string taut. I often draw my brims freehand – don't be afraid to do that too. Learn to use your eye.

✳ Not all fabrics will make good hats, so select your fabric with care. Each fabric will give a different result depending on its weight, thickness and stiffness. Very flimsy fabrics won't work well on their own unless you layer them over something more substantial such as interfacing. Very thick fabrics will also prove problematic. Keep an eye out for sturdy cottons, furnishing fabrics, lightweight tweeds, collar felt and so forth. You'll also need a lining, preferably something lightweight like cotton or calico.

✳ Do choose a washable fabric if you want a washable hat – and wash it before you use it. You don't want the fabric shrinking after you've put all the hard work in.

✳ Your hat's personality will change completely according to the fabric it's made from, so experiment and see what suits you!

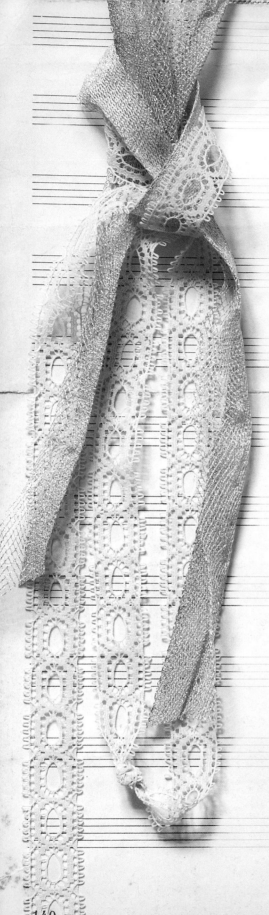

TO RUSSIA WITH LOVE

THIS HAT IS A GOOD ONE TO START WITH AS THERE ARE ONLY TWO PATTERN PIECES. IT'S MADE OF FAKE FUR, WHICH CAN HIDE A MULTITUDE OF SEWING SINS, AND WHAT'S MORE IT'S VERY WARM AND LOOKS TERRIBLY SOPHISTICATED. ON THE DOWNSIDE, FAKE FUR TENDS TO GET EVERYWHERE DURING THE MAKING PROCESS, AS I'VE LEARNED THROUGH EXPERIENCE.
  YOU DON'T NEED TO WORRY ABOUT CUTTING OUT THE FUR FABRIC ON THE BIAS, SO JUST DO IT ON THE STRAIGHT. HOWEVER, WHEN YOU'RE CUTTING THE FUR DO TRY TO CUT JUST THE WOVEN FABRIC BASE AND NOT THE FUR ITSELF AS OTHERWISE IT WILL END UP LOOKING CHOPPED – A BIT LIKE A BAD HAIRCUT!

YOU WILL NEED:

Measuring tape, ruler, compass, paper for your pattern and pencil

Scissors, pins, chalk, needle and thread

Fake fur fabric (you might need to buy half a metre – although you won't use that much)

Lining fabric

Sewing machine

BEFORE YOU BEGIN, MAKE THE PAPER PATTERN FOR YOUR HAT:

1. The side. First take your head measurement (h) using the method described in Basic Techniques (see page 20). Add on an extra 2cm for seam allowances. This gives you the length you'll need for the side of your hat. Now decide on the depth. I've made my hat 13cm deep, but again add on an extra 2cm for seam allowances – that's 15cm altogether. Now draw a rectangle on to paper using your own length and depth measurements (including your seam allowances). Cut out the rectangle and mark it CROWN/SIDE.

2. The top. Now you need to make the circular top for your hat. Use your original head measurement (h) without the extra 2cm for seams. Divide by 6.28, set your compass to this measurement and draw a circle on to paper.

3. Add on an extra 1cm all round for seams and then cut out the circle. Mark this CROWN/ TOP. Fold the circle into quarters and mark each quarter on the edge of the paper with little notches.

NOW TO MAKE UP THE HAT:

1. Pin both pattern pieces on to the wrong side of your fur fabric. Use lots of pins as it's quite tricky to cut this fabric out. Make sure you mark the notches on the crown. Cut out and then remove the pattern pieces. Cut out the same two pieces from your lining fabric (this time do make sure you place the CROWN/SIDE pattern on the bias of the fabric).

2. Now fold your CROWN/SIDE fur strip in half with right sides together and using a straight stitch, machine sew up the short seam with a 1cm seam allowance. Use a slightly longer stitch setting than normal as you're stitching fur fabric. Press the seam open with your fingers. You'll now have a wide tube. Fold the tube into quarters and mark the top edge with four little notches as illustrated.

3. With right sides together pin the fur CROWN/TOP to the top of the fur tube all the way round, matching up the notches. Machine stitch together using a straight stitch (again use a slightly longer stitch length for fake fur) leaving a 1cm seam allowance. If you prefer, you can tack these two pieces together first before machine stitching.

4. Repeat steps 2 and 3 with your lining fabric.

5. Now with right sides together pull your lining over your fur hat, matching up your centre back seams. Pin in place around the bottom and tack too if desired. Machine all the way round with a straight stitch 1cm from the bottom edge leaving a 10cm gap at the centre back. Take out any tacking stitches, then pull the fur through this gap so the hat's the right way out. Sew up the gap by hand, using slip stitch.

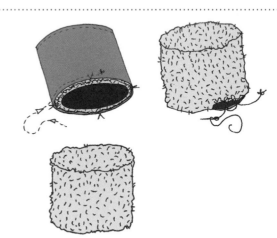

TWEED
TAM O'SHANTER

I'M HALF SCOTTISH, AND SO I'M A BIG FAN OF FAIR
ISLE JUMPERS, TARTAN TREWS, EIGHTSOME REELS
AND HIGHLAND TWEEDS! THIS VERY WEARABLE
BERET MAKES ME THINK OF CRISP ROMANTIC
WALKS IN BONNIE GLENS SPORTING 1940'S GARB.
IF YOU WANT TO GET INTO THE SWING OF THINGS
TOO THEN GIVE THIS TAM O'SHANTER A SHOT.

YOU
WILL
NEED:

Measuring tape, chalk, string
   and pencil to draw your circle,
   paper for your pattern
Scissors, pins, thimble, needle
   and thread
0.5 m lightweight tweed fabric
Separate lining fabric if desired
Sewing machine
Iron
Pompom

1. First you need to make a circular paper pattern for the top of your Tam. As this circle is large, use a pencil attached to a string to draw one or just draw round a large circular object instead. My circle had a 20cm radius. Cut out your pattern.

2. Fold your tweed fabric with the wrong sides together and pin your pattern into place. Cut out so that you have two circles. One circle will make the outside of your hat, and the other circle the lining. (If you want to make your lining out of separate fabric, then just cut out one circle from the tweed and one from the lining fabric and place the circles with wrong sides together as before.) Pin the circles together firmly and use your sewing machine to stitch them together all round the outside edge. It's best to use a zigzag stitch if you have one. This will stop any fraying when you gather up the edge.

3. Now to make the band for your Tam O'Shanter. Measure round your head and add on an extra 3cm for seams. Cut out a strip of tweed fabric on the bias this length x 7cm wide. Fold the strip with right sides together and sew up the short end so that the band fits round your head comfortably. Press the seam open. If you're worried about the sides of the band fraying as you work, then zigzag along them with the sewing machine too.

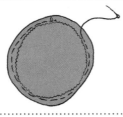

4. Thread a needle with a long double thread (a little longer than the length of your arm) and tie a knot on the end. Gather up the outside edge of your circle (see Basic Techniques page 24) and then start pulling up the thread until it's roughly the same size as the band. Don't tie off your thread yet.

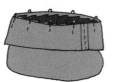

5. Now pin the right side of the band to the right side of your gathered circle, adjusting the gathers until they're even and fit into the band neatly. What I usually do at this point is to wrap my thread (and the dangling needle) around one of the pins so that I can carry on making little adjustments if needed.

6. Now tack the two pieces together, making sure you tack below the gathering stitches so that they won't show when you turn the Tam O'Shanter the right way out. Remove pins. Tie off your gathering thread at this point as it's done its job.

7. Now machine stitch with a straight stitch fractionally below your tacking line, and do this twice for strength. Remove tacking stitches and press the gathers downwards towards the outside edge of the band.

8. Turn up the band on the inside of your hat, folding over the top 0.5cm or so of fabric, adjusting until the band is the width you want it to be and covers all the gathers. Pin in place all the way round, easing and pressing the turn-up with your fingers as you go. Now slip stitch the inside of the band into place and remove the pins.

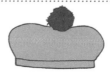

9. Finish your Tam O'Shanter off with a pompom – sewing it into the top layer only so that it doesn't mess up your lining.

BLOOMSBURY BELLE

THIS 1920'S-STYLE CLOCHE IS A RE-MAKE OF
ONE OF THE FIRST HATS I EVER DESIGNED.
IT'S A REALLY FLATTERING STYLE, AND
YOU CAN USE A VARIETY OF FABRICS TO GET
DIFFERENT EFFECTS – TWEED FOR WINTER,
CRISP COTTON OR LINEN FOR SUMMER.
IT CAN BE LEFT UNADORNED OR TRIMMED
WITH RIBBONS OR FLOWERS. THE HAT IS MADE
OF ONLY TWO PIECES AND IS SURPRISINGLY
STRAIGHTFORWARD. IT GETS ITS LOVELY BELL
SHAPE BY GATHERING UP THE FABRIC BY HAND.

YOU WILL NEED:

Measuring tape, ruler,
  compass, paper for your
  pattern and pencil
Fabric (allow 1m although
  you will use less)
Scissors, chalk, pins,
  needle and thread
Sewing machine
Iron
Polystyrene head
Lining fabric

FIRST MAKE YOUR PATTERN PIECES:

1. For the crown. Take your head measurement (h) using the method described in Basic Techniques (see page 20) and add on 2cm for seam allowances. Now draw a rectangle this length long and 20cm wide on to a piece of paper. Cut out and mark CROWN.

2. For the brim. Draw another rectangle 20cm wide and 90cm long on to your paper and cut out. Mark this BRIM.

TO MAKE YOUR HAT:

1. Pin the CROWN and BRIM patterns on to the right side of your fabric (both on the bias) and cut out. Remove patterns.

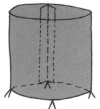

2. Take the fabric for the CROWN section and fold in half with right sides facing so that the short edges meet. Pin 1cm in from the short edge. Try on your head for size, adjust if necessary, and then stitch up the seam using the straight stitch on your sewing machine. Press the seam open. You now have a tube and this seam is the centre back. Turn the tube the right way out and mark the bottom edge of the tube with chalk so you remember which it is. Fold the tube into quarters and mark each quarter along the bottom edge with little notches as shown.

3. Now gather up the top of this tube about 0.5 cm in from the edge (see Basic Techniques page 24). Pull your thread as tight as you can without breaking it and secure with a knot. Stitch through the gathers a little with a separate thread to strengthen them. Press the top flat with your fingers. That's your crown made.

4. Fold the brim fabric in half with right sides facing so that the short sides meet. Leaving a 1cm seam allowance, sew the short edges together using the straight stitch on your machine. Press the seam flat using an iron. Turn the right way out.

5. Now fold this wide tube in half lengthways with wrong sides together and press. Secure and finish by sewing two parallel lines of straight stitches about 1cm in from the folded edge. Next fold into quarters and mark each quarter along the RAW edge with little notches as shown.

6. Either by hand or machine, put gathering stitches in along the raw edge of the wide tube about 0.5cm from the edge. Once you've done that, start to pull the stitches up. You'll see your brim start to form. Keep going until the brim is roughly the same size as the bottom of your crown. This takes adjustment and patience. When it looks about right, match up the back seams and the little notches, then pin the raw edge of the brim to the right side of the bottom edge of the crown as shown. Adjust the gathers so they're as neat as possible all round. When you're happy, tie off the gathers and tack the brim and crown together firmly all the way round just below the line of gathering stitches.

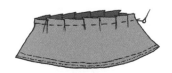

7. Machine stitch with a straight stitch all the way round right next to your tacking stitches. Remove the tacking stitches, turn the hat the right way out and press the seam up into the crown. Stitch again just above the seam line of the crown to give the hat a professional finish. Press.

8. To finish off, cut a small circle of fabric 6.5cm in diameter. Using a double thread, work a small running stitch around the edge by hand and gather up to create a puff. Use your fingers to flatten the puff down into a small circle – big enough to cover the little hole in the top of your hat. Tie off the gathering thread and pin the little circle in place on the hat. Slip stitch into place by hand. It can be helpful to do this on a polystyrene head.

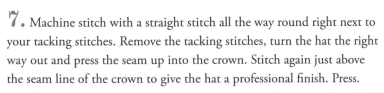

9. To line the hat, cut another crown pattern out of the lining material. Make up in exactly the same way as before, covering the little hole on the right side of the lining as in the previous step.

10. Finally, place the lining inside the crown of the hat with wrong sides together. Line up the back seams, fold over any excess fabric on the lining and pin in place. Slip stitch the lining into position by hand.

11. Place the finished hat on your polystyrene head if you have one and use the steam from your iron to smooth and even out the folds.

You can vary the look of this hat by making a larger brim, or by making the inside and outside of the brim in different fabrics. If you match the lining to the inside brim fabric, you'll have a reversible hat. Two for the price of one!

TRAVEL HAT

I LOVE COLLECTING WOVEN SOUVENIR BADGES AND THINK THEY LOOK GREAT ON HATS, SO I CALLED THIS THE TRAVEL HAT AS IT GAVE ME A GREAT EXCUSE FOR SHOWCASING THEM. I CAN JUST ADD MORE AS I MAKE MY WAY AROUND THE WORLD. THIS HAT IS MADE OF COLLAR FELT, WHICH COMES BY THE METRE AND IS ABOUT 3MM THICK. MAKE SURE YOU'RE NOT OFFERED THIN CRAFT FELT AS IT WON'T HAVE THE SAME FINISH. THIS THICKER FELT WILL GIVE YOUR HATS A GOOD FIRM FINISH, BUT IT'S ALSO SOFT ENOUGH TO PACK AND WILL JUST LOOK MORE VINTAGE IF IT GETS BASHED AROUND A BIT IN YOUR LUGGAGE.
  YOU CAN OF COURSE USE OTHER TYPES OF FABRIC TO MAKE THIS HAT, BUT THEY WILL COME OUT FLOPPIER. USE INTERFACING AS AN EXTRA LAYER IF YOU WANT A STIFFER FINISH. FELT DOES NOT NEED TO BE CUT ON THE BIAS, BUT IF YOU USE NORMAL FABRIC, YOU MUST PLACE THE CROWN/SIDE PATTERN PIECE ON THE BIAS.

YOU WILL NEED:

Measuring tape, ruler,
  compass, pencil and paper
  for your pattern
Scissors, chalk, pins,
  needle and thread
Collar felt (you'll need 1m
  of wide fabric)
Sewing machine
Iron
Lining fabric

TO TRIM:

Travel patches, leather lace,
  brooches, feathers

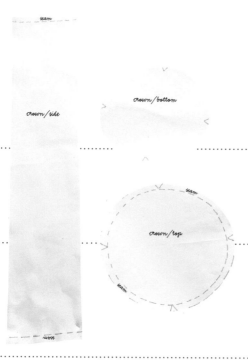

FIRST MAKE YOUR PATTERN PIECES:

1. *The side* First take your head measurement (h) using the method described in Basic Techniques (see page 20). Add on an extra 2cm for seam allowances. This gives you the length you'll need. Draw a rectangle this length long and 12cm wide on to a piece of paper. Cut out and mark this piece of paper CROWN/SIDE.

2. *The top* Next you need to make the circular top for the crown of your hat. Use your original head measurement (h) without the extra 2cm for seams. Divide by 6.28. Set your compass to this measurement, and now draw two circles this size on some paper.

3. Cut out the first circle just as it is and mark it CROWN/ BOTTOM. For the second circle, add on 1cm extra all round for seams, then cut out. Mark this CROWN/ TOP. Fold both circles into quarters and mark each quarter on the edge of the paper with little notches.

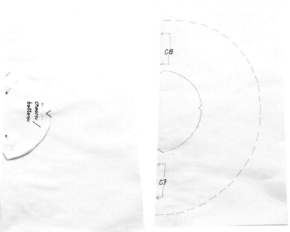

4. *The brim* To make the pattern for your brim take a large piece of paper or newspaper and fold it in half. Now take the paper circle marked CROWN/BOTTOM and fold it in half too. Pin it along the folded edge of the paper as shown. Trace around it (including the notches) then remove.

Draw half a brim shape around this circle. You can make the brim any size you like, but remember the bigger it is, the floppier it will be. The brim you see here is about 12cm wide at the front and back. Mark the pattern B for back and F for front. (CB = Centre Back / CF = Centre Front)

5. Once you're happy, put in a few pins to hold the paper together and cut out your brim. Now cut out the centre, making sure you put in the four notches that you've marked.

  NB If you need to make any adjustments to the shape of the brim once it's cut out, make sure you fold it back in half again as otherwise it won't be symmetrical.

MAKING UP THE HAT:

1. Pin your CROWN/SIDE pattern on to the right side of the fabric and cut out. If you're using felt, then you don't have to worry about the bias. If you're using other fabric, pin the pattern to the fabric on the bias. Mark the top of this strip with chalk so you remember which is the top and which is the bottom. Remove pattern.

2. Pin your CROWN/ TOP pattern on to the right side of your fabric (the bias isn't important here) and cut out. Cut little notches into the fabric where you marked the quarters on the pattern earlier. Remove pattern.

3. Place the remainder of your fabric with right sides together (the bias isn't important here) and pin the brim pattern in place really well. Cut out, remembering again to put the little notches in place to mark the centre, back and quarters on the inside of the brim. Remove pattern. (You'll have two brim pieces.)

4. Fold your CROWN/SIDE strip in half with right sides together and machine sew up the short seam using a straight stitch with a 1cm seam allowance. Press seam open. You'll now have a wide tube. Fold the tube into quarters so you can mark the quarters with little notches on both the top and bottom edges.

5. With right sides together pin the CROWN/TOP to the top of the tube all the way round, matching up the notches. Machine sew together using a straight stitch leaving a 1cm seam allowance. Repeat to add strength.

6. Clip seam all the way round and press downwards. I do this by making a pad out of an old tea towel so that I can get it inside the crown of the hat. I can then press against it with the iron.

7. To neaten, machine sew a line of straight stitches (using a slightly longer stitch setting than normal) just below the seam of the crown as shown. Press again.

8. Pin the brim pieces with right sides together firmly and machine sew with a straight stitch all the way around the outside about 0.5cm from the edge. Do this twice for strength. Clip the seam and then turn the brim the right way out and press carefully.

9. Machine sew (using a slightly longer stitch setting than normal) with a straight stitch around the outside edge of the brim about 1cm from the edge to finish it off neatly.

10. Now pin the right side of the crown and the brim together matching notches, and making sure the seam at the centre back of the crown lines up with the centre back of your brim. Machine sew with a straight stitch all the way round twice for strength. Keep an eye on the layers to make sure they stay flat as you're sewing. It's easy to get the crown caught in on itself. Neaten the seam with scissors when finished and press the hat as best you can.

11. Trim the hat by sewing on your travel patches by hand. I also added a leather lace, some brooches and a feather!

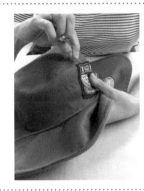

12. To line the hat make another crown in your lining fabric. Place the lining inside the crown as shown with WRONG sides of the fabric facing, matching up centre back seams. Fold over any excess lining and pin in place around the hat. Slip stitch the lining into position by hand, taking care not to let your stitches show on the outside of your hat.

Collect together souvenirs from your travels and use them to individualise your hat.

A ROOM
WITH A VIEW

IT'S A RIDICULOUSLY ROMANTIC NAME FOR A
RIDICULOUSLY ROMANTIC-LOOKING HAT. IN SPITE
OF ITS ARISTOCRATIC ASSOCIATIONS HOWEVER, THIS
HAT IS A REAL BARGAIN. MADE OUT OF UNBLEACHED
CALICO AND SOME BEAUTIFUL FOUND LACE, I MADE
IT FOR VIRTUALLY NOTHING. USE SIMILAR MATERIALS
AND YOU COULD BAG YOURSELF A BARGAIN TOO.
 MAKE THE BRIM AS LARGE OR AS SMALL AS YOU LIKE.
MINE IS A VERY GENEROUS 20CM AT THE FRONT AND
14CM AT THE BACK. USE A MEDIUM WEIGHT INTERFACING
TO GIVE IT SOME BODY AS IT WILL BE TOO FLOPPY
OTHERWISE, ESPECIALLY IF YOU MAKE A LARGE BRIM.
THE PRECISE LOOK OF THE HAT WILL DEPEND VERY
MUCH ON THE FABRICS YOU USE. REMEMBER TO WASH
YOUR CALICO FIRST TO PRE-SHRINK IT.

*This hat, like all
the cut and sew
hats, is designed
for those with some
stitching experience
but this is probably
the trickiest in
the section as it
uses a number of
different skills.*

YOU WILL NEED:

Measuring tape, ruler, compass,
  pencil and paper for your pattern
Scissors, chalk, pins, needle and
  thread
Fabric for your hat
  (I used 1m of wide calico)
Medium weight interfacing
  (non-iron and woven if possible)
Sewing machine
Iron
Bias binding (2.5cm wide and long
  enough to go around the edge of
  your brim)
Some lace to decorate your hat
Lining fabric (I simply used the
  calico again)

FIRST THE PATTERN:

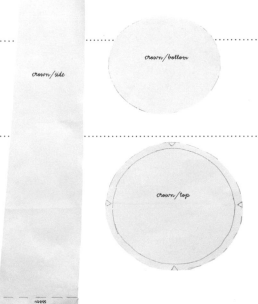

1. *The side* First take your head measurement (h) using the method described in Basic Techniques. Add on an extra 2cm for seam allowances. This gives you the length you'll need. Now cut out a paper strip 12cm wide x this length. Mark it CROWN/SIDE.

2. *The top* Next you need to make the circular top for the crown of your hat. Use your original head measurement (h) without the extra 2cm for seams. Divide by 6.28. Set your compass to this measurement, and now draw two circles this size on to your paper.

3. Cut out the first circle just as it is and mark it CROWN/ BOTTOM. For the second circle, add on 1cm extra all round for seams before cutting out. Mark this CROWN/ TOP. Fold the CROWN/ TOP circle into quarters and mark each quarter on the edge of the paper with little notches as shown. Open out.

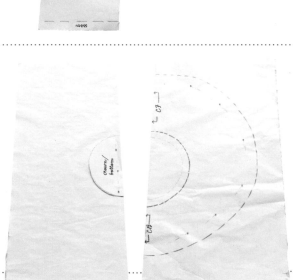

4. *The brim* To make the pattern for your brim take a large piece of paper or newspaper and fold it in half. Now take the paper circle marked CROWN/BOTTOM and fold it in half too. Pin it along the folded edge of the paper as shown. Trace around it then remove. Now draw another circle 2cm out from the traced line as shown. This is the line you will use to plan your brim so mark it clearly with a thick pen. Carefully draw half a brim shape around this thick circle. My brim was smaller at the back (14cm) and larger at the front (20cm) but you can make yours any size you like. Mark CF for Centre Front and CB for Centre Back on the folds of the pattern.

5. Once you're happy with the shape, put in a few pins to hold the paper together and cut out your brim. Now cut out the centre too along the thick line.

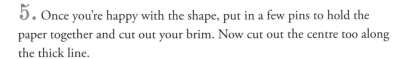

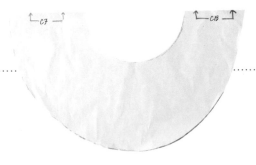

6. Next, cut along the fold at the Centre Back of your pattern. Hold the pattern around your head at the place where your hat would normally fit, and pinch the paper together at the back so that the brim fits snugly as shown sloping gently downwards. You might need a friend to help you do this. Make sure you have equal amounts of paper on each side and put in a pin where the paper meets. Now put in a line of pins. Try on again to ensure you've got the right fit. Cut the paper as you can see here 1cm out from the pins. Take out the pins and open out the pattern.

NOW MAKE UP YOUR HAT:

1. Pin your CROWN/SIDE pattern on to the right side of the fabric on the bias and cut out. Mark the top of this strip with chalk so you can tell the top from the bottom. Remove pattern. Cut out another strip from interfacing if you want a firmer finish.

2. Pin your CROWN/ TOP pattern on to the right side of your fabric (don't worry about the bias) and cut out including notches. Remove pattern. Cut out another top exactly the same from interfacing.

3. Place the remainder of your fabric with wrong sides together and pin the brim pattern in place on the bias. This brim MUST be cut on the bias to help give it shape. Cut out and remove pattern. You'll have two brim pieces. Now cut out a brim in your interfacing too.

4. Take your CROWN/SIDE strip of fabric and place the interfacing strip on to the wrong side of it. Now fold the combined strip in half with right sides of the fabric together and pin together the short side.

5. Machine sew up the short seam using a straight stitch with a 1cm seam allowance. Press seam open. You'll now have a wide tube. Fold the tube into quarters and mark them with little notches along the top edge.

6. Take your CROWN/TOP and place the interfacing top on to the wrong side of it. Now, with right sides together pin the combined CROWN/TOP to the top of the CROWN/SIDE tube all the way round, matching up the notches. Machine sew together using a straight stitch leaving a 1cm seam allowance.

7. Clip the seam all the way round and press downwards. I do this by making a pad out of an old tea towel so that I can get it inside the crown of the hat. I can then press against it with the iron.
To neaten, machine sew a line of straight stitches (using a slightly longer stitch setting than normal) just below the seam of the crown as shown. Press.

8. Now for the brim. Place your interfacing brim on top of the wrong side of one of your fabric brims. Hold together with pins. Fold the brim in half with right sides of the fabric facing, and machine sew up the side seam using a straight stitch and a 1cm seam allowance. Now sew up the side seam of the remaining fabric brim in the same way.
Press all seams open.

9. Make a brim sandwich so that the interfacing is in the middle and the right sides of the fabric face outwards. Pin together firmly. Machine sew a line of stitching all the way around the outer edge 0.5 cm in. Trim the edge if necessary when done to make sure it's even.

10. Take your bias binding and measure the length you need to go all around the outside edge of your brim. Fold the bias binding in half and ease around the brim and tack in place. Now set the straight stitch on your machine to a slightly longer setting, and machine sew parallel lines of stitching all the way around the brim. This keeps the layers together but also adds decoration and shape. Tack the raw edges of the brim together at the head fitting.

11. Using the longer straight stitch on your machine sew your bias binding into place and remove tacking stitches.

12. Join the crown to the brim by pinning right sides together, matching the Centre Back seam lines. You can tack the two pieces together first if you wish before machine stitching together using a straight stitch. Clip the seam (see page 28).

TO FINISH:

Pin the lace into position and try on your hat in the mirror. When you're happy, stitch the lace on to the hat by hand using tiny stitches on the surface, pushing your needle along through the layers of the brim so that any long stitches in between don't show. Work on small sections at a time. You'll be surprised at how quickly you manage to do this. To line the hat make another crown in your lining fabric. Place the lining inside the crown with WRONG sides of the fabric facing, matching up centre back seams. Fold over any excess lining and pin in place around the hat. Slip stitch the lining into position by hand, taking care not to let your stitches show on the outside of your hat.

DECORATE YOUR HATBOX

ONCE YOU START MAKING FABULOUS HATS, YOU'LL NEED TO STORE THEM PROPERLY. HATS CRUSH EASILY AND WILL SOON START TO LOSE THEIR FRESHNESS IF NOT LOOKED AFTER WELL. KEEP THEM FROM HARM BY STOWING THEM IN PRETTY HATBOXES NESTLED IN LOTS OF CRUMPLED-UP TISSUE PAPER. IF YOU WANT TO MAKE YOUR OWN VINTAGE-STYLE HATBOXES OR REVAMP UNSIGHTLY ONES THEN FOLLOW THIS SIMPLE BUT EFFECTIVE DÉCOUPAGE METHOD.

YOU WILL NEED:

Newspaper
PVA glue and a brush
Old magazines
Plain cardboard hatbox
Bradawl
Length of wide striped
    ribbon

1. Lay down some old newspaper to protect your work surface and dilute your PVA with water until it's the consistency of fairly thick single cream.

2. Rip up your old magazines.

3. Paste your ripped-up magazines on to the hatbox, coating liberally with PVA as you go. You can do it completely randomly, just make sure you paste your paper over the sides of the boxes and the lids too so that there are no raw edges. Continue to paste magazine pieces on the inside covering all surfaces completely. Allow to dry thoroughly.

4. Mark two holes in your hatbox just below the lid area. The holes need to be exactly opposite each other. Use a bradawl to make the holes and then thread your ribbon through, securing on the inside with large knots.

Hatboxes are ideal for travel too of course. I have a couple of smaller ones, more like vanity cases, which are perfect for stashing my little headpieces in if I'm heading off on a jaunt.

Keep your eyes peeled for original vintage hatboxes — not only do they protect your hats, they look fantastic stacked on top of one another around the home.

Look out for little vintage hat stands on which to display your hats as well. They're so cute! You can still find them on eBay and at flea markets.

Old-fashioned coat hooks and hat racks are perfect for displaying your hats, and make great storage for hats and coats.

DECORATED HEADS

You can also apply découpage to the polystyrene heads used in the book to make them into something much more attractive for display purposes. Decorated, these heads are perfect for showcasing your hats around the home.

Use the same method as for the hatboxes, but with smaller pieces of paper, especially around the nose eyes and mouth. I used fabric instead of paper on some of my heads too and this worked equally well. Remember to apply découpage around the bottom of the neck so there are no raw edges on show.

I always prefer to rip my paper and fabric rather than cut it — it gives a more vintage and appealing look.

Best of all, check out auction-rooms for bargain sets of antlers — they make a quirky home for your hats and quite a statement.

INDEX

SUPPLIERS

THERE ARE A GROWING NUMBER OF EXCELLENT MILLINERY SUPPLIERS OUT THERE, SO DO SEARCH THE INTERNET AS THERE'S ALWAYS SOMETHING NEW POPPING UP. HERE ARE A FEW OF MY OWN FAVOURITES. MOST ARE ONLINE AND OFFER A MAIL ORDER SERVICE.

Barnett Lawson Trimmings
London, UK
www.bltrimmings.com
Millinery wire, feathers, trims, ready-made hat shapes, fascinator bases, headbands, veiling, crin, buttons and all manner of other goodies.

Baxter Hart & Abraham
Luton, UK
www.baxterhart.co.uk
Friendly efficient service. Felt and straw hoods, fascinator bases, feathers, peterhsam ribbon, sinamay, and all sorts of other millinery supplies.

The Berwick Street Cloth Shop London, UK
www.theberwickstreetclothshop.com
At the heart of London's fashion fabric district. Sells collar felt (Travel Hat pages 152–157) and cotton organdy (Pretty Petals pages 88–91) as well as a wide variety of other unique fabrics.

Boon and Lane Ltd
www.hatblockstore.co.uk
The number one destination for hand-crafted hat blocks. Worth a visit just to step back in time.

MacCulloch and Wallis
London, UK
www.macculloch-wallis.co.uk
A good source of hard-to-find millinery foundation materials such as millinery buckram and interfacings.

Morplan
www.morplan.com
The place to find polystyrene display heads for either practical or decorative purposes.

Parkin Fabrics Ltd
Oldham, UK
www.parkinfabrics.co.uk
Great all-round millinery supplier with huge variety of stock.

The Trimming Company
(online only)
www.thetrimmingcompany.com
Big online supplier of millinery goods. Reasonably priced wide variety of feather trims.

Wayward
St Leonards-on-sea, UK
www.wayward.co/
The shop is out of this world and so is the stock! An amazing place for tracking down vintage haberdashery. The owners also run a market stall on Portobello Road in London.

And if you want to learn how to create your own vintage looks to compliment your hats may I recommend:

Miss Honey Bare
www.misshoneybare.com
She's the stylist for the wonderful looks in this book.

Lynsey Le Keux
www.lekeuxevents.co.uk
She's given me lots of vintage hair and make-up tips in the past.

TEMPLATES

ORGANDY FLOWERS: LONG THIN ELEGANT PETAL PATTERN

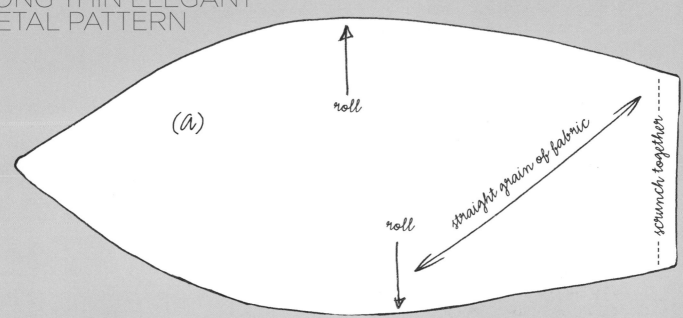

(a)

roll

roll

straight grain of fabric

scrunch together

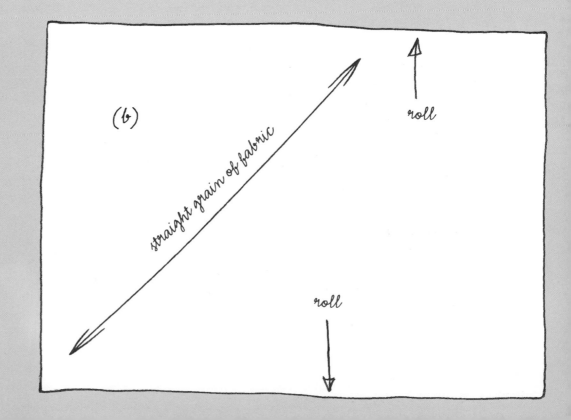

(b)

straight grain of fabric

roll

roll

Large

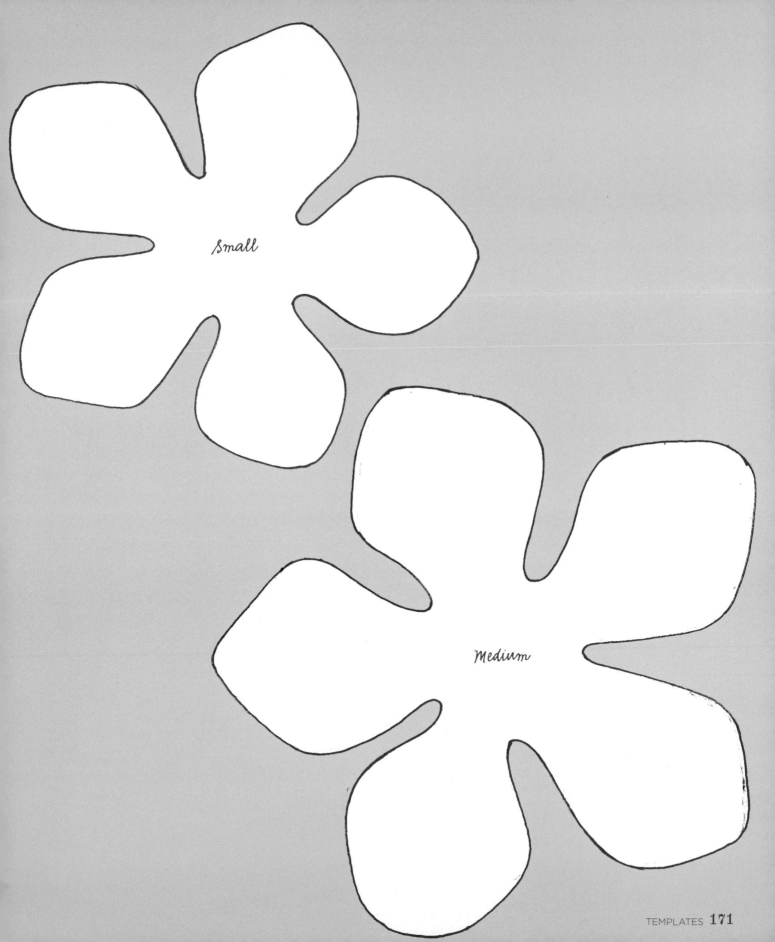

Small

Medium

BONDAWEB
FLOWERS

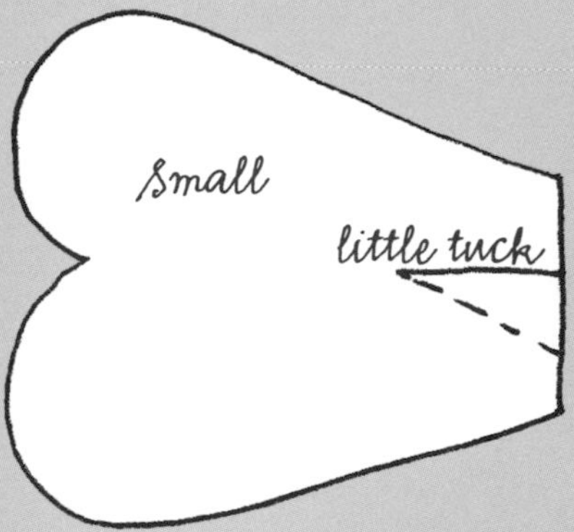

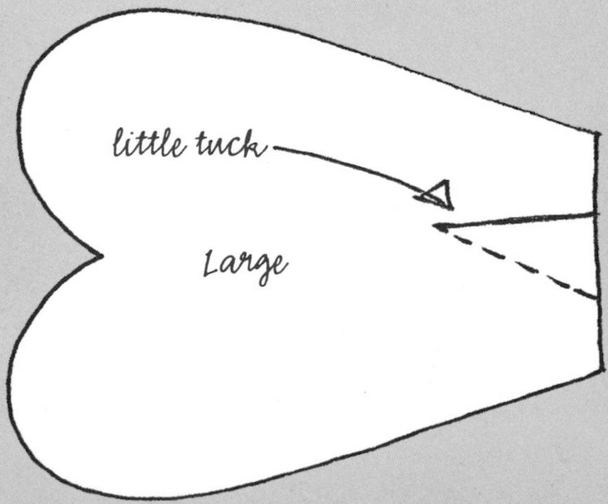

Small

little tuck

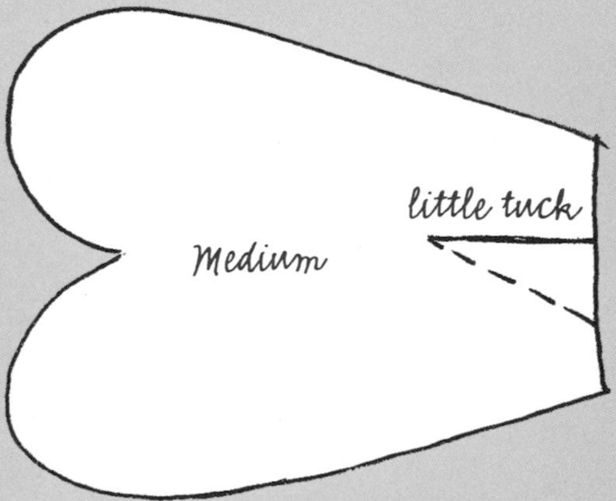

Medium

little tuck

little tuck

Large

BEAUTIFUL
BOW
HEADPIECE

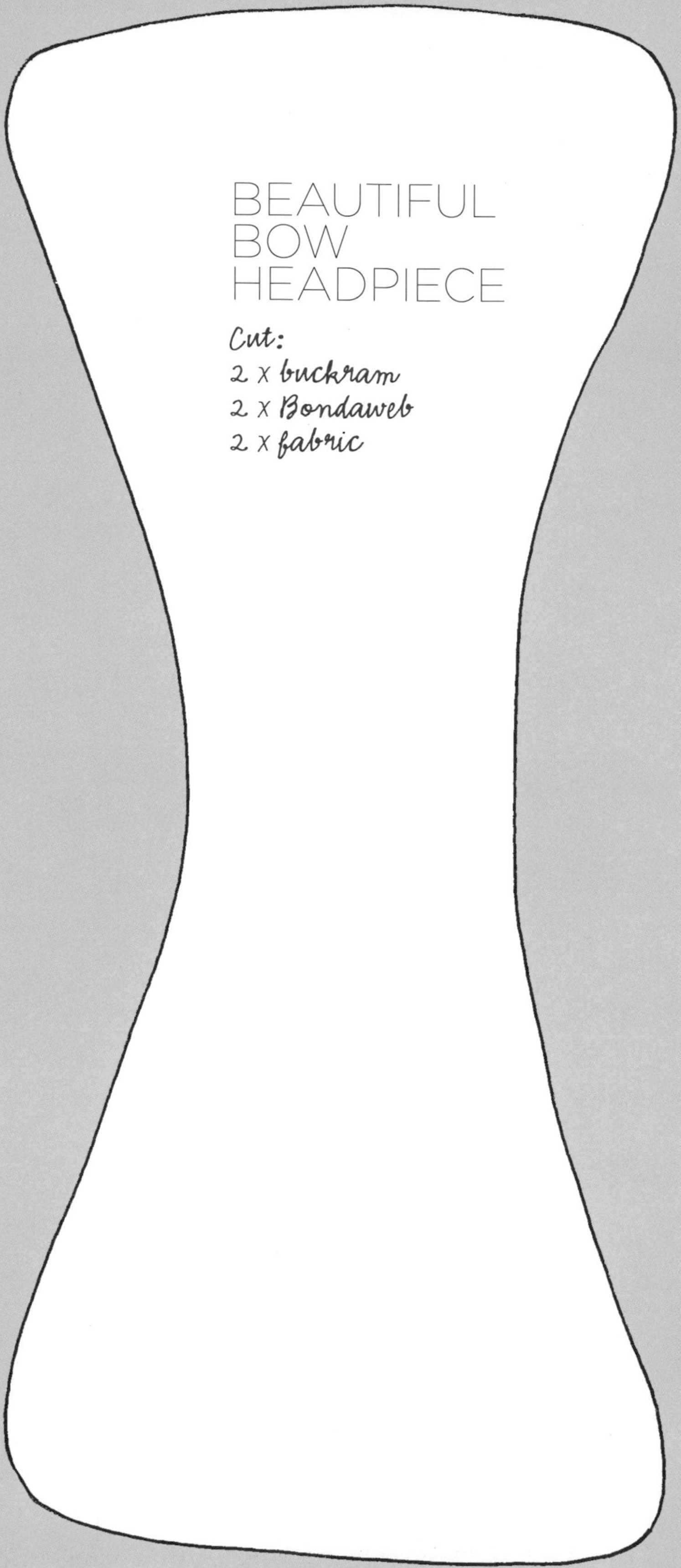

Cut:
2 x buckram
2 x Bondaweb
2 x fabric

TEARDROP

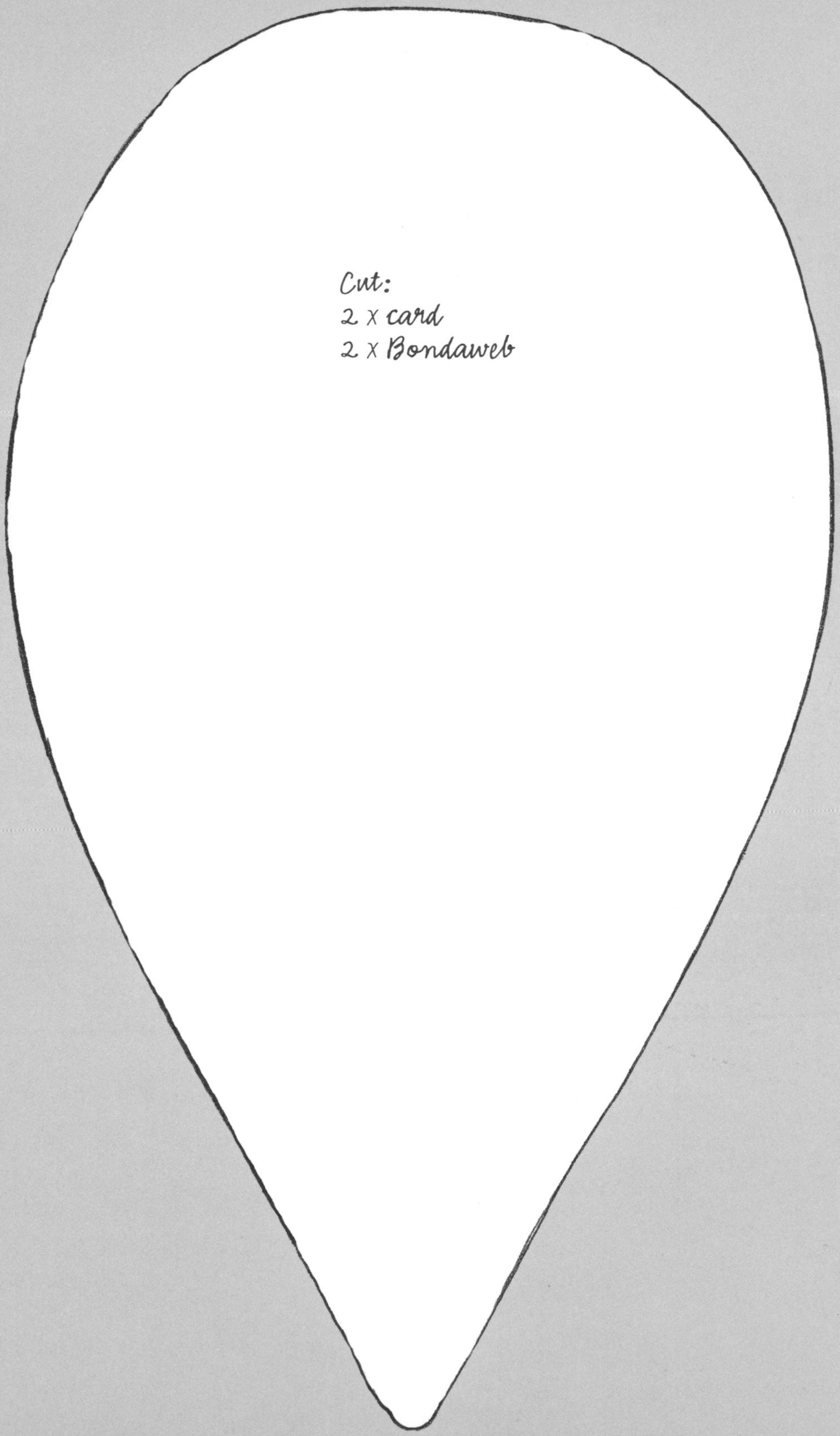

Cut:
2 x card
2 x Bondaweb

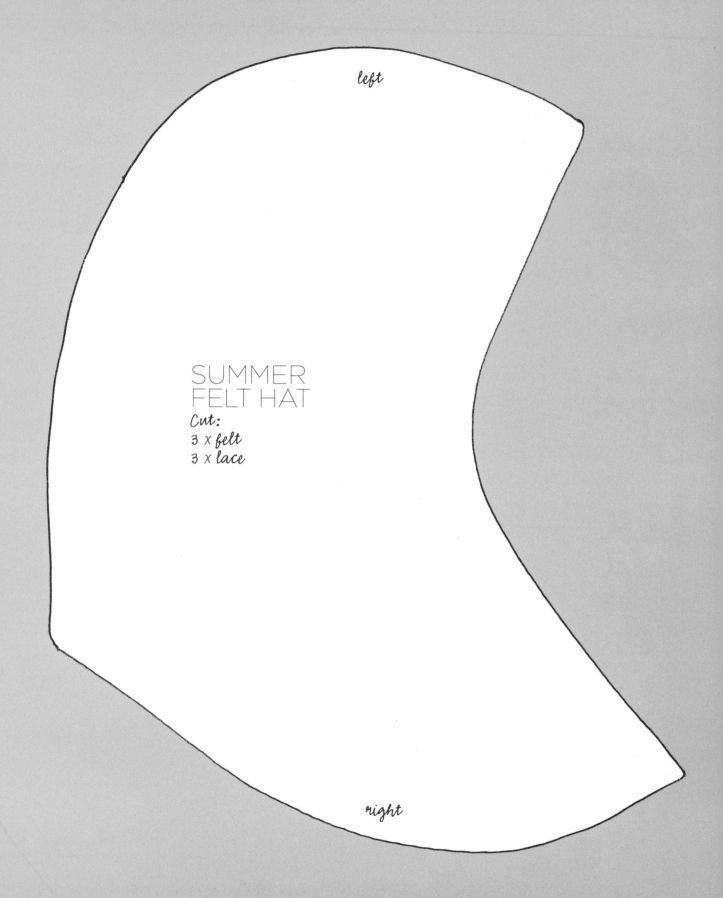

left

SUMMER
FELT HAT
Cut:
3 x felt
3 x lace

right

SUMMER FELT & BOW FOR SPARKLY MINI BERET

For summer felt cut:
1 x felt
1 x lace

For beret cut:
1 x felt
2 x fabric

Thank you very much

Hats off to the many faithful friends, colleagues and members of my family who've been such a constant source of support and encouragement. A special mention for Sandra and John Westbrooke who helped keep me sane and also proofread my book.

I'd also very much like to thank Sarah Hosking and the Trustees of The Hosking Houses Trust (www.hoskinghouses.co.uk) which offers residencies and bursaries to women writers. Sarah, my time with you helped kick-start the creative process and your personal enthusiasm was an unexpected and treasured gift.

Claire Richardson not only took the amazing photographs for the book but also organised the whole of our fabulous hat shoot in Hastings - even setting up much needed massages for frazzled writers and fish & chips on the beach! Her lovely assistant Amy Barton kept us all smiling and on track. Talented stylist Leida Nassir-Pour

(whose shop Warp & Weft in Hastings is a must-visit) provided the wonderful vintage clothes and created the magical mood for the book whilst Miss Honey Bare (www.misshoneybare.com) devised the fabulous hair and make-up looks for our stunning models – Felix, Savannah, Rosie, Alice and Kiera.

My book designer Helen Bratby is a creative superstar and a joy to work with, and heaven knows how I'd cope without the calm coaxing of my editor Sophie Allen. Huge gratitude too to Esther Coombs (www.esthercoombs. com) whose wonderful quirky images are right up my street. What a dream team! I loved working with you all. Thank you so very much for making my vision a reality.

In addition warm thanks to Nicola Jackson who loaned us her lovely flat in St Leonards for the day and kept us going with teas and coffees. I'm

grateful too to Shaun Brosnan, who not only allowed us to use his fabulous Old Rectory (www.theoldrectoryhastings. co.uk) but also lent us his prized Alfa Romeo Spider Veloce. What a darling! And to Deb Bowness for loaning us her beautiful wallpapers.

Our ice-cream van came courtesy of the West Hill Café in Hastings, and I'll always remember our wonderful morning shooting at the haberdashery heaven that is Wayward in St Leonards (see suppliers).

Finally a big heartfelt thank you to my agent Clare Hulton and the staff at Kyle Books for their support and conviction.

…..and I want to give a special hug to Ninja – my neighbour's cat for just being a fabulous four-footed friend!

Mary Jane x